A Simple Model of Discipleship
Following Jesus in Love, Trust, and Fear

Kevin Rogers

A Simple Model of Discipleship: Following Jesus in Love, Trust, and Fear
Copyright © 2020 by Kevin Rogers

All rights reserved. No part of this book may be reproduced or used in any manner without the prior written permission of the copyright owner, except in the case of brief quotations in book reviews or articles. To request permission, please contact:
Kevin Rogers at wkevinrogers@gmail.com

ISBN 978-1-7357813-1-0 (paperback)
ISBN 978-1-7357813-2-7 (hardback)
ISBN 978-1-7357813-0-3 (e-book)

Unless otherwise indicated, all Scripture quotations are from the ESV® Bible (The Holy Bible, English Standard Version®), copyright © 2001 by Crossway, a publishing ministry of Good News Publishers. Used by permission. All rights reserved.

Scripture quotations marked (NIV) are taken from the Holy Bible, New International Version®, NIV®. Copyright © 1973, 1978, 1984, 2011 by Biblica, Inc.TM Used by permission of Zondervan. All rights reserved worldwide. www.zondervan.com The "NIV" and "New International Version" are trademarks registered in the United States Patent and Trademark Office by Biblica, Inc.TM

Scripture quotations marked (NKJV) are taken from the New King James Version®. Copyright © 1982 by Thomas Nelson. Used by permission. All rights reserved.

First printing in 2020
Printed in the United States of America

*To my church family for the past fifteen years,
with deep thankfulness to God for you all.*

*For I long to see you, that I may impart to you some
spiritual gift to strengthen you—that is, that we
may be mutually encouraged by each other's faith,
both yours and mine. – Romans 1:11–12*

Chapters

Introduction. A Simple Model of Discipleship 1

1. What is Discipleship? 9

2. What is Love? 20

3. What Does It Mean to Love God? 32

4. What Does It Mean to Love Other People? 40

5. What Does It Mean to Trust God? 48

6. What Does It Mean to Fear God? 59

7. What about Growing in the Knowledge of God? 70

8. How Do We Grow in Love for God? 82

9. How Do We Grow in Trust in God? 112

10. How Do We Grow in Fear of God? 128

11. How Do We Grow in Love for Others? 146

Conclusion. Until the Kingdom Comes 163

Personal Reflection and Small Group Discussion Guide 168

Acknowledgments 184

Introduction

A Simple Model of Discipleship

If I were to share a simple model for good physical health with you, it might go something like this:

Eat well.

Exercise consistently.

Get enough sleep.

Get regular checkups.

We'd call this a simple model for a couple of reasons. First, it's a *model* in that it's an attempt to take something complicated and boil it down to its primary parts or principles so it's easier to understand. A model isn't exhaustive—there are a lot of details it doesn't speak to. How exactly should I prepare my meals in order to "eat well"? What kind of exercise do I need to do and for how long? How much sleep is enough sleep? And which doctors do I need to see regularly? This is a model in that it doesn't try to address the specifics as to how all this works in each and every situation related to physical health. Second, this model is *simple* in that it's easy to understand. Even a child could grasp what each of these points means.

Yet, despite its simplicity, this a powerful model, isn't it?

A simple model like this helps us to understand the most important things about a particular subject or concept. It enables us to get our arms around the question "What is this?" In this case, the question we can grasp quickly is "What does it take to have good physical health?"

A simple model like this also helps us evaluate our lives. In this regard, a model leads us to answer the question "How am I doing?" When I see the model above, I immediately start to ask myself questions like "Am I getting enough sleep?" and "How many times did I exercise last week?"

Finally, a simple model like this helps us set priorities and make decisions. It helps us answer the question, "What do I need to do?" As I look ahead to the next three months and think about what I need to do to stay healthy, the model reminds me of the importance of regular checkups. Recalling that my last regular checkup for skin cancer was canceled, I pick up the phone to call and schedule a visit with the dermatologist.

A simple model like this can take you a long way toward enjoying physical health even though you need to work out how to apply these principles specifically to your own life.

I believe there is a parallel to this simple model for good physical health when it comes to Christian discipleship. There's a simple model rooted in the Bible that will help you get your arms around the concept of discipleship, evaluate where you are as a disciple, and determine what you need to do to grow as a disciple. Just like our model for good physical health, this simple model of discipleship is easy to understand, even though it's still a lifelong struggle to live out. This model also doesn't say everything there is to be said about discipleship. There are still a lot of specifics to work out in individual lives and congregations. But for all of that, it's a powerful model for understanding what discipleship is, for growing as disciples, and for making disciples of others.

What is this simple model? It's this:

To be a disciple of Jesus means to follow him by growing in love, trust, and fear of God and in love for other people.

That's it.

Why I've Written This Book

In 2008, I was still fresh out of seminary. I hadn't been serving at our church as an elder for very long (and didn't have the gray hair that gives credibility to that title for me today). When I got word that the Christian organization I was working for had decided to bring a nationally known pastor to speak to us, I was excited. I anticipated an insightful message and a challenge rooted in God's Word. I wasn't disappointed. What I didn't expect, though, was the unusual epiphany I would experience that day.

Our speaker's message was on Matthew 28:19–20, Jesus's Great Commission. In case you're not familiar with this short passage, it's at the very end of the book of Matthew. In his final words on earth before ascending to his Father in heaven, Jesus gives his closest followers the mission they are to carry out going forward:

> Go therefore and make disciples of all nations, baptizing them in the name of the Father and of the Son and of the Holy Spirit, teaching them to observe all that I have commanded you. And behold, I am with you always, to the end of the age.

"It's crystal clear, isn't it?" said our speaker. "The one thing Jesus tells his church to do is to make disciples. And yet, how often are we tempted to do everything except the one thing that Jesus told us to do?" *True*, I thought, *on both counts.*

"A significant part of the problem," he went on to say, "is that we are perplexed about how to make disciples. I've spoken to groups of church leaders and asked that question—How do we make disciples?—and have

Introduction ▪ 5

gotten a room of blank looks in response." If he had looked at my face at that moment, he would have seen a blank look there too.

It's strange to describe that moment as an epiphany because that term usually describes a moment when the lights come *on*. You suddenly understand something clearly that you didn't understand before. I did have an epiphany that day, but it was unusual in that what became clear to me was that there was something foundational to Christianity that I didn't understand. The lights came on that the lights were *off*. I had been a Christian for ten years and studied at a seminary for four of those years. But at that moment, I realized that I had little idea about how to make disciples or even to define exactly what a disciple is. At the same time, I felt an urgent reminder that making disciples was the primary mission Jesus left for his church. And I was a church leader who was almost completely in the dark about it! I thought, *If we as church leaders don't know specifically what a disciple is or how to go about making disciples, how is the church as a whole going to carry out its mission?*

I knew, of course, that the ultimate success of the church doesn't rest on human leaders. Jesus himself made that very clear when he said, "I will build my church" (Matt. 16:18). Despite human ignorance (or lack of clarity, if we want to put it more mildly), Christ is at work growing his church. Yet this doesn't discount the fact that—just as in many other areas of life—knowledge, wisdom, and skill matter. Even an ignorant gardener can put some tomato plants in the ground and have a harvest, but the wise gardener will almost always have fruit that is healthier and more plentiful—not to mention that an ignorant gardener can do severe damage to a plant that would have flourished otherwise. In the same way, knowledge and wisdom matter when it comes to making disciples who thrive and reflect Christ beautifully.

That day, I began to look for answers to my questions about discipleship. The answers I sought didn't come quickly or easily. I thought there would be books that would make it all clear (I had thought the same thing about parenting books too), but I never found them. The answers only came after years of pondering and through the ups and downs of life and ministry. Looking back, I think a book like this one would have been beneficial to me, and that's why I've written it. This book aims to provide you with some clear, concise, and straightforward answers about discipleship so you can flourish as a disciple of Jesus and help others grow as well.

Perhaps you are a new Christian who wants to grow in your faith, but you aren't sure exactly how to go about doing so. It seems like you know so little and there's so much to learn. You feel intimidated because you've heard so much advice about what you need to do to grow as a Christian. You'd love to have some clarity and

Introduction ▪ 7

simplicity when it comes to understanding how to live as a Christian. This book is for you.

Perhaps you are a Christian who is wrestling with what discipleship means for you. You realize how vital discipleship is and want to ensure that you are moving toward the mark that Jesus has set for you. But that mark seems a little abstract, and you're not sure if you're even making progress. This book is for you.

Perhaps you are a ministry or small group leader in your church. You have zeal to serve Christ and to see the group you lead grow in Christlikeness, but when it comes to the specifics of making this happen, you're in the dark. This book is for you.

Or perhaps you're a pastor, and as you've read these introductory paragraphs, you sense a blank look coming over your face. You clearly see that (a) the church's mission is to make disciples, and (b) you don't have a specific idea of what you are aiming for or where you need to begin. As I've said, I've been there. This book is for you.

Finally, perhaps you're not a Christian yourself, but you're interested in learning more about Christianity. I hope that this book will be a help to you as well. I especially hope that it will convey a distinct idea of the life that God calls all people to in and through Jesus Christ. As Christians, we readily admit that it's a life we tarnish by our human sin and failings, but it is still a beautiful life indeed.

The Plan

If this model is so simple, then why do I need to write a whole book about it? That's a good question.

The answer is that some justification for this simple model is needed. That's the first chapter. There I talk about the basics of discipleship and why this simple model is sufficient to serve as a basis for our lives as Christians.

But as it turns out, the various aspects of this simple model aren't quite as easily understood as a statement like "get more exercise." We all know what that means, of course. But there's a lot more confusion when it comes to understanding specifically what it means to love or fear God. Chapters 2 through 6, therefore, are devoted to clearly explaining each of the four aspects of the simple model—what it means to love God, trust God, fear God, and love other people.

Finally, after we've understood exactly what each of these concepts means, we need to turn our attention to the question of how we grow in love, trust, and fear, and how we can help others grow as well. That's why I've written chapters 7 through 11. Then I finish with a chapter that, hopefully, serves to turn our gaze to the glorious end of the road of our discipleship and why it's important to fix our eyes there.

Chapter One

What is Discipleship?

Christine is a new Christian, eager to move forward in her newfound faith in Jesus. She's just gotten connected with a large church in her area, and she's looking through the church's website to get to know all the pastors' names. There's the lead pastor—she's heard him speak a few times, so she recognizes him. Then there's someone who is the pastor of families and another who is the pastor of counseling. She thinks it's great that the church has pastors to meet these important needs. But as she scrolls to the bottom of the page, she sees one more pastor—the pastor of discipleship. *I wonder what he does*, she thinks to herself.

The following Sunday there are announcements at the end of the worship service. Everyone seems enthusiastic, but none more so to Christine than the women's ministry leader. She has a big announcement, she says, one that is going to play a significant role in the spiritual lives of the women in the church. She says, "This fall, we're forming discipleship groups for the women of this church. Anyone who wants to be involved can sign up at the table in the lobby." Christine sees little pockets of ladies near her murmuring excitedly. One of the ladies catches Christine's eye, expecting her to be excited as well, so Christine gives her a sheepish smile. She's too embarrassed to ask the question she's sure everyone else knows the answer to: "What's a discipleship group?"

A month later, Christine is at one of the church's midweek small-group gatherings. It meets close to her house, and she's enjoyed getting to know some of the church's members better over the last few weeks. The leader of her small group is a pretty intense guy, but she likes that—he's challenging in a good way. The past week he challenged the group to read through the entire Gospel of Matthew—four chapters per day to finish all twenty-eight chapters in seven days. And the whole group did it! As Christine read throughout the week, she had been struck by that same word, the name that Jesus's followers were called time and again—*disciples*. As her small-group leader wraps up the discussion for the night, he references the "Great Commission" at the very end of Matthew's Gospel. "The Bible makes it clear," he says, "that the concept of discipleship is at the heart of what it means to be a Christian and at the heart of what we are to do together as the church."

As Christine has learned, you don't have to be in a church long before you hear the term "discipleship." And for good reason—the concept is found throughout the New Testament. Discipleship is important; all Christians know that. But the question is… what exactly is it?

What Is Discipleship?

Discipleship is the process of growing as a disciple of Jesus. I know this definition violates a cardinal rule: you can't use the same term in the definition you're trying to define (*discipleship* means growing as a *disciple*). But bear with me. I'm going to elaborate on the term disciple shortly. For now, I don't want you to miss the first point I want to convey, namely that: Discipleship is a process of growing.

Some words that end in "-ship" imply an unchanging condition, but this isn't true of discipleship. For instance, discipleship isn't like membership. The moment I became a member of my local YMCA, I became as much of a member as I'll ever be. I was able to sign up for all the classes and use all the equipment available to members, and I had to pay my dues just like all the other members (while telling myself, like the rest of them, that soon I'll be working out all the time). I never "grow" as a member. To be a member of a gym is a static thing—nothing ever changes as far as being a member goes.

That's not true when it comes to discipleship, though. Yes, there are some similarities. Once you truly become a disciple, you always remain a disciple. And all disciples stand before God on equal footing: the righteousness of Jesus Christ, which God credits to us as a result of our faith in him. But there is also a vital difference—membership is a static thing, but discipleship is a dynamic thing. To be a disciple is to *grow*.

In our churches, sometimes we use the word "discipleship" to speak of our own growth as a disciple, and sometimes we use it to speak about training others as disciples. But in either of those cases, at the heart of the matter is the process of growing as a follower of Jesus. This process is what we're looking to understand further, then. How do we grow as disciples? How do we help others grow as disciples? But before we can do that, we have to first understand what it means to be a disciple of Jesus.

The Need for Specifics

Most of the teaching I've heard on the broad topic of discipleship starts by framing the conversation around two big questions:

1. What is a disciple?
2. How do we make disciples?

The discussion that ensues usually follows a similar pattern. First, there's a short answer given to the first question: a disciple is a follower of Jesus. Since this answer is almost universally agreed on, not much time is spent discussing it. One thing often made clear is that "following" Jesus means learning from him in order to be like him. And that's exactly right, as we learn from Jesus's words in Luke 6:40: "A disciple is not above his teacher, but everyone when he is fully trained will be like his teacher."

Once the teacher affirms that a disciple is someone who follows Jesus to be like him, the discussion quickly moves on to the second question, which gets the rest—and the lion's share—of the discussion: "How do we make disciples?"

These two questions are indeed the right questions (though we need to insert "How do I grow as a disciple?" between them to address the full picture of discipleship), but this approach moves too quickly. It's not enough to say that a disciple is a follower of Jesus. To really understand what it means to be a disciple, we need to ask, "In what particular ways are we to follow Jesus?" Should all of us seek to become itinerant teachers? Should we spend our lives in the same places in Israel that he did? I'm not trying to be irreverent or ridiculous. I'm simply making the point that there's a question here that needs to be answered.

But isn't it enough to say that we are to follow Jesus in "Christlikeness"? No, it's not—at least not until we understand in which ways we are to be like Christ. While noting that a disciple is "to be like Christ" is correct, it's no more specific than saying that being a disciple means "following Christ." Before we move on to the question of how to make disciples, we need to know what we are specifically aiming for as disciples so we can more effectively grow toward that goal and help others grow toward it as well.

The Heart of the Matter

A Christian disciple is indeed a follower of Jesus. That definition is short and succinct and yet as broad as an entire life. And because the reality of following Christ encompasses a Christian's entire life, the concept is so large that we have trouble getting our arms around it. This is perhaps our biggest challenge when it comes to understanding discipleship. It's like deciding that we want to know everything about insects (put yourself in the shoes of a young boy for a moment) and then hearing that there are 5.5 million species of insects in the world. The topic is so large that you don't know where to start. Likewise, how can we possibly be specific about the ways we are to follow Jesus without giving a pages-long answer covering all the different aspects of Jesus's life we are to imitate?

There is a way. And we discover this way by focusing not on Jesus's words or actions but rather on the motivations of his heart. Doesn't this intuitively seem right? Before discipleship is ever about following Jesus in the sense of doing what he did, it is about following Jesus in the sense of having the same attitudes of the heart, the same motives, and the same desires as he did. As the Bible makes clear, our words and actions always flow out of what's in our hearts (Matt. 12:34–35). Here's how we get a concise yet comprehensive answer to the ways we are to follow Jesus: we can trace the source of the Lord's words and actions back to a small number of "foundational motivations" in his heart.[1]

These foundational motivations are like the taproot of a tree. The taproot is a large, dominant root that usually grows straight down, anchoring the whole tree. The taproot is significant because all the other roots of the tree sprout from it. If you have a big tree in your yard, there are probably different places, yards away from one another, where a knobby root pokes up out of the ground. But if you exposed the tree's root system, you would see that all these roots can be traced back to the taproot.

While a tree only has one taproot, for the sake of illustration I want to make the case that there were four "taproots" in the Lord's heart—four big foundational

---

1   I call these "foundational motivations" for lack of a better, single word to describe them. There isn't one category to group these terms under that seems satisfactory to me—whether "attitudes" or "emotions" or "religious affections" or even simply "motives." None of them seems to rightly capture all these motivations. Thus, I call them foundational motivations simply because they motivated the Lord to do what he said and did and were foundational in the sense of being primary sources of motivation on which everything else was built.

16 ▪ *A Simple Model of Discipleship*

motivations out of which "grew" all that he said and did. By identifying these taproots, we're able to identify the specific ways in which we are to grow more and more like Jesus. I posit that everything in the life of the Lord Jesus Christ ultimately flowed out of one of these four foundational motivations: love for God, trust in God, fear of God, and love for other people.

I don't believe any Christian would argue that Jesus didn't possess each one of these four foundational motivations. A short trip into the Scriptures makes it clear that each of these filled his heart.[2] But I do understand why someone would wonder if we can really trace all that the Lord said and did back to these four motivations. Aren't we missing something?

From my own study and from pondering the question at length, I can only answer this way: I don't think so.

I know this is a significant claim. Rather than attempting to prove this now, though, I want to ask you to bear with me as I make my case throughout the book. As I elaborate on what it means to love, trust, and fear God and to love other people, it will become clear how

---

2   Love of God: "But I do as the Father has commanded me, so that the world may know that I love the Father" (John 14:31); Trust in God: "And going a little farther he fell on his face and prayed, saying, 'My Father, if it be possible, let this cup pass from me; nevertheless, not as I will, but as you will'" (Matt. 26:39); Fear of God: "In the days of his flesh, Jesus offered up prayers and supplications, with loud cries and tears, to him who was able to save him from death, and he was heard because of his reverence" (Heb. 5:7). "Reverence" here is essentially "fear;" Love for others: "Greater love has no one than this, that someone lay down his life for his friends" (John 15:13).

we can trace everything in the Lord's life—his words and actions, his emotions and attitudes—back to these four foundational motivations.

The Missing Practices

So far in this chapter, we've covered the questions "What is discipleship?" and "What is a disciple?" We've also looked at what it really means to follow Christ: by making the motivations of his heart the motivations of our hearts.

But there is still a lingering question I need to address before moving on: What about all the things we are to *do* as disciples? It seems there are so many specific ways we are to follow Christ, so many specific practices we are called to do—praying, encouraging other Christians, or evangelizing, just to name a few. Yet this model doesn't address any of those things. This is a good question, especially since we usually talk about these practices whenever we're discussing discipleship. And most books on discipleship spend a considerable amount of time focused on these various practices. Why don't I mention them then?

It's not because these practices don't matter—of course they do. Rather, it's because all these practices are "downstream" from loving, trusting, and fearing God and loving other people. As in Jesus's life, the four foundational motivations are the fountainhead of all other aspects of discipleship. Everything we do as disciples ought to ultimately flow from them.

Evangelism provides a clear example of this. The way we become increasingly evangelistic is by growing in our love for God (so that relishing his beauty compels us to tell others about him) and by growing in our love for others (so that we are increasingly willing to tell them what is good for them even if we lose their esteem or face retribution for it). When we love God more and love people more, we will share the good news about Jesus more. So what we need to do is aim to love God more, trust him more, fear him more, and love other people more. The other practices will (super)naturally follow.

I am not arguing that there's no need to talk about these various spiritual practices. In fact, I'm going to talk about them to some extent when I answer the question of how we grow as disciples, because these practices not only flow out of love, trust, and fear but they also help love, trust, and fear to grow. But I think that discussing all the details of how to go about reading your Bible or evangelizing your neighbors is best saved for week-to-week life in the local church, in the same way that no model for good physical health would detail all the various ways you should prepare your vegetables. My aim, again, is to share a model of discipleship that is comprehensive but concise—a simple model.

But this is only a simple model if we clearly comprehend what it means to love, trust, and fear God and to love other people. As simple as our model of physical health seems, if we don't understand what "exercise" is

Chapter One ▪ 19

or what a "checkup" is, our model isn't going to help us get healthy. Likewise, if we don't understand what it means to love, trust, and fear God, and to love other people, this model isn't going to help us grow as disciples. There is great confusion in our culture and—it must be said—in our churches when it comes to each of these things.

With that in mind, we now turn our attention to understanding those foundational motivations more clearly.

Chapter Two

What is Love?

What is love? For those of us who were teens in the 1990s, that question inevitably elicits a musical response—the voice of an anguished Haddaway belting out the question from his smash single, "What Is Love." (If you're like me, you may need a few moments now for that bass line to finish in your mind before you continue reading.) Unfortunately, though we listened to him ask the question countless times, Haddaway never gave us an answer. Like us, he seemed utterly perplexed about the whole notion. He just knew that he wanted love but was afraid of being burned by it.

By and large, it seems we're still there—we know that life without love is empty, and we know that love carries with it the possibility of great pain, but all the while we have trouble articulating exactly what love is.

Isn't it astounding that we have such trouble defining a word we use so commonly and is so important to our lives?

This is also true in the church. Love is obviously important to Christians and the Christian life. At the heart of our understanding of the nature of God is the affirmation that "God is love." According to Jesus, the greatest commandments given in God's law are to "love the Lord your God with all your heart and with all your soul and with all your mind" and to "love your neighbor as yourself" (Matt. 22:37, 39). Throughout the New Testament, we find encouragements and admonitions to love everyone from our fellow church members to our enemies. Yet, though the word "love" is used often in our worship services and in conversations among Christians, there is no clear and commonly shared understanding of what love is. (If you need further evidence that this is true, answer the question yourself. Then ask a couple of Christian friends what love is and compare answers.)

With regard to how we as Christians understand love, a significant part of our problem is that we commonly think and speak of love as one simple thing—not simple in the sense of being without complications, for we all know that love is complicated. What I mean is that when we are speaking about our love for God or our love for our neighbor or our love for our family, we tend to think of all these loves as one simple thing we call "love." While we might speak of Christian love and talk about how this is different from the love we find out in the world, we still tend to think of all Christian love as one and the same love, whether God's love for us, our love for God, or our love for one another in the church. Then, as we attempt to understand what love is, we try to wrap our arms around the characteristics of all these various loves to get at a single definition. It's no wonder we have trouble defining love.

But here's an important truth, one that I think helps provide clarity: while we often think and speak of love as one thing, love is not one thing—it's two things. That is, there are two different loves, each with a different nature. So what we really need—to start, at least—is two different definitions of love.

"Affection" Love

Love is, in one sense, *really, really liking someone or something*. That's not a very technical definition, but it's the best way to communicate this first definition of love. We like salad, but we love chocolate. We like vegetables, but we love pizza. We like our coworkers, but we love our spouses. Love is, if you will, at the far end of the scale beyond "like" in the same way that "hate" (in this sense) is at the opposite end of the same scale beyond "dislike."

If we wanted to put it a little differently, love in this respect is our hearts' inclination toward someone or deep fondness for something. That which we love we think about, daydream about, delight ourselves in, and enjoy as often as we can.

It is what we love in this sense of the word that determines how we live our lives. If I love golf (and I do), I don't just watch golf on television. I also talk with my friends about the tournament that finished up the weekend before. I go to the driving range to practice. I might even pick up a club and go into the backyard to take a few practice swings. I play whenever I get the chance. And then I think about and savor the best shots I hit. The next day will likely find me slipping into daydreams about being out on the course again. This is what it means to love golf—to have my heart so taken by it that it fills my life.

But since some of you equate watching golf with Sunday afternoon naps, let me give you another example. My wife loves to cook. It's not merely the process of preparing food that she likes; it's also seeing the people she loves sitting down at the table together to enjoy a delicious meal. Because she relishes this, she thinks long and hard about our menu for the week. She subscribes to food and cooking magazines and is excited when they arrive in the mail. She's always on the lookout for new recipes that will introduce new flavors and favorites to the family, or that will improve a dish that is already a favorite. She takes classes to learn more about preparing various foods so that the end product will be even better. Her love for cooking affects her life profoundly. Anything we really love—whatever it is—does the same.

There is a tendency in Christian circles to downplay affection love. It's often considered (at worst) merely worldly or (at best) not as important as the type of divine love that sacrifices for others. This is a mistake. After all, God himself loves this way, so it's divine too. When he looked down at Jesus being baptized, God the Father said, "This is my *beloved* Son, with whom *I am well pleased*" (Matt. 3:17, emphasis added).

The Father's heart is full of joy, adoration, and gladness in his Son, whom he *loves*. God created human beings in his image with this capacity for affection love, and he intends for it to be fulfilled.

For the record, it's not merely our experience but rather the Bible itself that points us toward this two-fold definition of love. For those of us who see God's Word as the ultimate definition of what is true, we want to ensure that our definition(s) of love correspond to the definition(s) we find in the Bible. Throughout the Scriptures, we find the word "love" used to convey a sense of deep affection for someone or something. Consider Jacob's love for his bride-to-be, Rachel:

> Laban had two daughters. The name of the older was Leah, and the name of the younger was

Rachel. Leah's eyes were weak, but Rachel was beautiful in form and appearance. Jacob loved Rachel. And he said, "I will serve you seven years for your younger daughter Rachel." Laban said, "It is better that I give her to you than I should give her to any other man; stay with me." So Jacob served seven years for Rachel, and they seemed to him but a few days because of the love he had for her. (Gen. 29:16–20)

Jacob delighted in Rachel's beauty so much that he was willing to be a servant for seven years to make her his wife. And that love was so great that the seven years seemed like nothing. If we are using the Bible as our bedrock of what is true, we see that it defines love (in one sense, at least) as deep affection.[1]

To recap, then, one way to define love is to say that it is the delight or relish that we have in someone or something. Note that I've used, and will continue to use, several different terms—"affection," "fondness," "delight," "relish"—synonymously to capture that sense of enthrallment of the heart.

---

1 For another example, consider 1 John 2:15: "Do not love the world or the things in the world." In this passage, "the world" is referring to the collective anti-God attitude, desires, and culture of fallen humanity. We are being instructed in this passage to *not* love the world. John is saying, in effect, "Do not let your hearts be drawn to delight in and relish those things in the world around you that stand opposed to God's wisdom, word, and holiness."

26 ▪ A Simple Model of Discipleship

"Resolve" Love

On December 4, 2006, a nineteen-year-old American soldier named Ross McGinnis was in the gunner's hatch of a Humvee in Baghdad, Iraq. Four other soldiers were riding down in the body of the vehicle when a grenade, thrown by an insurgent from above, dropped past McGinnis and into the truck. McGinnis had time to leap out of the Humvee and save his own life. Instead, he dropped into the vehicle, yelling to his comrades that the grenade was inside. When he saw it lodged near the radio, he pinned it down with his body. It exploded, and McGinnis's body absorbed most of the force from the blast. One of the other soldiers was significantly injured, but all four of them survived. McGinnis was killed instantly by the blast.

At the ceremony posthumously awarding McGinnis the Medal of Honor, President George W. Bush remarked that the young soldier was being rightly honored for going beyond merely doing his duty to exemplifying the greatest love that one person can demonstrate to another: giving his life for the lives of others. Who among us would disagree?

When we speak of love, we aren't always speaking of really liking someone or something. There is a second type of love. The definition of that second type of love is *a joyful resolve for the good of another person.* Unlike affection love, this type of love is not as commonly or easily understood, but the Scriptures help make it clear for us. One of the best places to go to understand this type of love is Romans 13:8–10. This is what the apostle Paul writes there to the church in Rome:

> Owe no one anything, except to love each other, for the one who loves another has fulfilled the law. For the commandments, "You shall not commit adultery, You shall not murder, You shall not steal, You shall not covet," and any other commandment, are summed up in this word: "You shall love your neighbor as yourself." Love does no wrong to a neighbor; therefore love is the fulfilling of the law.

Paul writes, in effect, "The only thing you should 'owe' each other is love for one another. If you love one another, you will fulfill God's law. All the other commands he has given—don't commit adultery, don't commit murder, and so forth—are simply what it means to love your neighbor as yourself."

What type of love is Paul speaking of here? Is it simply affection love? No, this is a different kind of love. It's a love where the primary focus is not on *our* feelings (like affection love) but rather on the good of *other* people. It's a love that isn't about who or what we like but instead about the benevolent attitude and actions we take toward our neighbors, regardless of who they are.

It's verse 10 that makes the nature of this type of love clear: "Love does no wrong to a neighbor." This is a negative definition, saying what love is not, but it also elucidates what love is. If love does no wrong to a neighbor, it must always do the opposite—love always acts for the *good* of its neighbor. The love that Paul writes about in Romans 13 is a resolve to act for the good of other people.

Love Is Joyful

But there is one more word we need to highlight. Our definition of this resolve type of love is that it is a *joyful* resolve to do good for another person. To truly be love, there must be gladness in it.

This is what makes love different from mere duty. Duty says, "I am obligated to do good to another; therefore I will fulfill this obligation regardless of how I feel." But love goes further than duty. Love says, "I am glad to do good for another." This gladness can still be mingled with tears at the cost of love—think of Jesus in the garden of Gethsemane. He was in agony and experiencing deep grief, yet we know he still had gladness—the Scriptures tell us that "for the joy set before him he endured the cross" (Heb. 12:2 NIV).

Resolve love, then, is not devoid of emotion. Love is only love when it is carried out with gladness. Even if it's not outwardly expressed, this love brings happiness to the heart when doing good for another. And it is a far greater happiness that we can experience if we only seek our own good, for it is happiness doubled, tripled—a joy that's multiplied by the joy of countless others.[2]

Again, when we speak about love in the second sense, we think particularly of our commitment or resolve to do good to others. Even when it is costly to us, love means we are committed to doing—gladly doing—what is good for others.

So there are two different types of love, and never the twain shall meet, right? Well… not quite.

How These Loves Become Love

I started this chapter by saying that love isn't one simple thing. And it's not. It's two simple things—affection love and resolve love. But there is still a challenge when it comes to understanding love. Not only do we speak of affection as love and of the joyful resolve for the good of others as love, but these two types of love often come together in varying degrees to form another concept that we commonly call love. Think about it— your love for your parents or your spouse and children

---

2 It's this love of joyful resolve to which Christians refer when they speak of "agape love" or "unconditional love" as divine love ("*agape*" is one of the Greek words used in the New Testament for "love"). While I don't think that "agape love" is the best term for this type of love (since "agape" is used also in the New Testament to express affection love), it does help highlight an important truth: this type of love speaks of who God is. When the Bible says, "God is love," what does that mean? It means that day after day, moment after moment, God is joyfully seeking the good of others.

is a combination of affection love and resolve love. It's not merely one or the other. We could say that love is two simple things or one compound thing. No wonder there's a lot of confusion about love!

Love is like water. There's hot water and cold water and varying temperatures in between. Hot and cold water are distinct, yet both are water. Hot water by itself is water, and cold water by itself is water. Yet put the two together, and you have... water. The same is true of love. Think of affection love as "hot water" love and resolve love as "cold water" love.[3] We call either of those on their own love, but we can combine the two and call it love as well.

It's easy to think that one "temperature" of love is better than the other, but that's not true. Certain temperatures of love are appropriate for certain relationships in the same way that certain temperatures of water are appropriate in certain circumstances. No one working in the heat in the middle of summer asks for a drink of hot water. And almost no one getting into a shower in the middle of winter would say that cold water is always best. It all depends on the circumstances—or, in the case of love, on the particular relationship.

---

3   Calling resolve love "cold water" love does not mean that it's devoid of emotion or emotionally "cold," a misconception that has already been dispelled. The designation is simply to distinguish resolve love from affection love within this analogy of love as water.

Chapter Two ▪ 31

I share this analogy comparing love to water for a couple of reasons. First, I think it's necessary because we are trying to describe the reality of love—the way that we use the term and the way we experience it. To simply say that love is not one but two things is too simple. It doesn't fully explain the way we use the word "love." We need to understand how love can be two different things and at the same time a combination of those two things.

But just as importantly, I share this analogy as a way to understand two very specific loves—love for God and love for other people.

Chapter Three

What Does It Mean to Love God?

What does it mean to love God? There's really no overstating the importance of this question. If that sounds like an exaggeration, consider Matthew 22:35–38. In this passage, Jesus responds to a weighty question from one of the experts of God's law, which he had given to the people of Israel through Moses:

> And one of them, a lawyer, asked [Jesus] a question to test him. "Teacher, which is the great commandment in the Law?" And he said to him, "You shall love the Lord your God with all your heart and with all your soul and with all your mind. This is the great and first commandment."

Chapter Three ▪ 33

To love God is the great and first commandment. Let your heart weigh that for a moment. The greatest obligation, the foremost requirement, laid on us as human beings by God is to love him. But what exactly is this love for God?

One Possible Answer

One answer to this question from well-versed (and well-intentioned, no doubt) Christians is that loving God is simply obeying God. Love for God, then, would primarily be the impulse to obey God. This understanding stems from 1 John 5:3: "For this is the love of God, that we keep his commandments." That seems pretty plainly stated, doesn't it? *This* is the love of God, that we keep his commandments. Isn't it clear here that love is essentially obedience?

Before answering too quickly, though, listen to what the same author (the apostle John) writes elsewhere in the Bible. In John 14:15, he records that Jesus told his disciples, "If you love me, you will keep my commandments." Here, it's clear that love for Jesus exists prior to keeping his commands. Love for Jesus is one thing; if it's present, then obeying Jesus (another thing) will follow.

In light of the latter verse, I take 1 John 5:3 to mean that love for God is so inextricably bound up with obeying God that it's not possible to even consider love for God to be genuine if there is no obedience to God.[1] But they're not one and the same. Love for God always results in obedience, but love for God is not the same thing as obedience.

What Temperature Is This Love?

Think again of our analogy of love as water. When we turn on the tap, we might turn on the hot water, or we might turn on the cold water. Or we might turn on both the hot and the cold to get some temperature in between. In the same way, when we speak of love, we might mean affection love or resolve love (or some combination of the two). What "temperature" should our love for God be? Is it only hot (affection love) or cold (resolve love)? Or is it some temperature between the two?

When we come to understand that God is our Father, a natural conclusion might be to think that our love for God is essentially the same love we have for our human parents. Along with respect for them, we usually feel a love that is equal parts affection for the love they have shown us and a resolve to do whatever good we can for them, making for a temperature of love that's right in the middle.

But while there is some similarity between the love we have for our parents and the love we are to express to

---

1   First John 5:2 supports this distinction between love and obedience as well: "By this we know that we love the children of God, when we love God and obey his commandments."

God, it's not an exact parallel. When we have trusted in Christ, we are adopted as a child of God and thus enter into a relationship with him. God the Father becomes *our* Father. Given that this is true, it is certainly the case in some sense that we love God with resolve love. That is, we love God in the sense of joyfully seeking his good. Because God has adopted us as his children in Christ, he has opened himself up, so to speak, to be gladdened or hurt by us. And in this sense, of course, to love God means that we are resolved to think and speak and live in a way that brings him joy, not grief.

But in another sense, we can't do anything for God's good—it's impossible. There is nothing that God needs from us (or anyone!) and nothing he doesn't have that we can give to him. "He is not served by human hands, as if he needed anything," as Paul makes clear to the Athenians in Acts 17:25 (NIV). So, while there is some part of our love for God that is resolve love, it's a comparatively small part.

This leads us to the conclusion that *our love for God is primarily to be the love of affection or delight.* If there's only a little room for us to love God in the sense of joyfully seeking his good, the command to love God must largely be a command for us to delight in him. The temperature of the water of our love for God then is to be very, very warm – not strictly affection love, but almost exclusively that.

But is this the way we see love for God portrayed in the Bible? I believe it is.

The Bible on Love for God

For starters, consider the command of Psalm 37:4: "Delight yourself in the LORD." We've said that affection love is really delighting in someone or something. Here, the psalmist is essentially saying, "Love the Lord with the love of affection!" While this might not be everything there is to say about what it means to love God, it's certainly significant that we have a clear command in the Bible to love God in this sense of affection love.

But a richer, more poetic picture of love for God is also painted in one of the lesser-known books of the Old Testament, the Song of Solomon. This short book is a love poem between a young bride and a young groom. When you stop and think about it, it makes you wonder, "What's that doing in the Bible?" I mean, the Bible is about God and our spiritual life, so why is there a love poem there? And this isn't a "My love is like a red, red rose" poem to be read by the local ladies' garden club as they sip their afternoon tea. It's a poem with enough not-so-subtle erotic imagery in it to guarantee you won't be reading it aloud at the youth retreat. So why is it in the Bible?

The Song of Solomon is there for us to know that God heartily approves of these two lovers who are completely taken with one another. They see one another's beauty and are deeply enamored with the sight. They relish one another. It's a picture of affection love in full bloom. It is, assuredly, a poem that highlights the glory of marital love and an encouragement for all married couples to strive for that ideal.

But there is also a long history in the church of interpreting the book as a representation of the spiritual relationship between Jesus Christ and the church—the King and his bride. Both interpretations, it seems to me, are legitimate; there's a double meaning to the book. But if that is true, what does that imply about what our love for God (or here, the Son of God) ought to be like? It's obvious, isn't it? We are to be intoxicated with the beauty and glory of God. Our hearts are to relish him and be full of affection for him.

The Love of a Lover

Our love for God, at its best, is to be the affection of someone who is deeply in love—a lover.[2] He can't stop thinking of how beautiful she is, the way she smiles, the way she laughs. In a real sense, what he is getting out of the relationship is far greater than what he is giving to the relationship. Yes, I know that if he is a true love, then he will do anything for his beloved

---

2 Some men might read this and think, "All this talk about romantic love—that's a feminine thing." Nothing could be further from the truth. We've already made this point: I love golf, my wife loves cooking—everyone loves *something*. It's tragic for someone to think that being masculine means to love football or NASCAR or guns or cars more than the living God. That's not manly. It's just foolish. Not to mention that David, perhaps the preeminent lover of God in the Bible outside of Jesus himself, was a warrior who had killed bears and lions in close combat.

and does indeed seek to do her good. But isn't it the case that even giving his life seems like a small price to pay compared to the greatness of his love for her, his delight in her? The point is that affection love is far more about what's happening in our hearts, while resolve love focuses primarily on what is done for the good of the other person. In this, too, our love for God is like that of the lover.

One other important point to make in this regard is that our love for God is to be like love for another *person*, not for an abstract *thing*. God is not a thing— he is a personal being. We don't love God in the way we love a piece of beautiful art, admiring its characteristics from afar. The love of God is delight in all God is while being rooted in a personal relationship with him. And because we are in a relationship with God, it also means that our love extends to all God has done, is doing, and will do for us. We delight in and adore God for who he is, and we delight in and adore all the good he has done for us, especially the great good he has done for us in Christ.

Jonathan Edwards, the great American theologian, captured love for God succinctly in this way: "'Tis the soul's relish of the supreme excellency of the Divine nature, inclining the heart to God as the chief good."[3]

---

3 Jonathan Edwards, *Treatise on Grace and Other Posthumously Published Writings* (Cambridge: James Clarke, 1971), 49.

Love for God is indeed a relishing—a savoring—of the beauty and glory of who God is and what he has done, and it moves us to seek to know him more. It is a response to seeing God and really, really liking what we see.[4]

When the Bible speaks of our love for God, it primarily refers to this love of affection. So, when we speak of growing in our love for God, this is essentially what we are asking: How do I grow in my delight in the beauty of God? How do I grow in my deep joy, my relishing, of who he is and what he has done for me?

---

4 Theologians from the past spoke of this type of love as *complacence* (a term that was used differently than how we use it today). Jonathan Edwards explains it succinctly: "What is commonly called love of complacence, presupposes beauty. For it is no other than delight in beauty; or complacence in the person or being beloved for his beauty" (Jonathan Edwards, "A Dissertation on The Nature of True Virtue," in *The Works of Jonathan Edwards*, ed. Edward Hickman [Edinburgh: Banner of Truth, 1974, orig. 1834], 1:123). What I've termed "affection love" is essentially the complacence Edwards writes about—a delight in beauty.

Chapter Four

What Does It Mean to Love Other People?

If you've ever been to a wedding in America, especially a Christian wedding, you probably heard these words from the Bible at some point during the ceremony:

> Love is patient and kind; love does not envy or boast; it is not arrogant or rude. It does not insist on its own way; it is not irritable or resentful; it does not rejoice at wrongdoing, but rejoices with the truth. Love bears all things, believes all things, hopes all things, endures all things. (1 Cor. 13:4–7)

While it's not technically a poem, it is poetic, and Christians and non-Christians alike esteem it as one of the most beautiful statements about love ever penned. Though it's not specifically about romantic love, it's still good for marrying couples to hear and heed because it's this type of love that fuels the fire of romantic love over a lifetime.

Patience, kindness, refusal to envy or boast, not being arrogant or rude, and not insisting on our own way all point to a love that focuses on other people. This gets to the heart of the type of love we are to show to others. *Our love for other people is the love of joyful resolve for their good.* While the love for God we are designed for (and commanded to) is largely the love of affection, delight, and relish, the love for (most) other people we are commanded to display is at the other end of the temperature scale. It is straight-up cold water—the love of joyful resolve for the good of others.

How the Bible Makes This Clear

Toward the end of the Sermon on the Mount, Jesus lays down the Golden Rule: "So whatever you wish that others would do to you, do also to them, for this is the Law and the Prophets" (Matt. 7:12). While the actual Golden Rule is well known ("Whatever you wish that others would do to you, do also to them"), the last part of this verse is not ("for this is the Law and the Prophets"). What does that mean?

The Law and the Prophets are divisions of the Hebrew Scriptures (Old Testament). But the phrase "the Law and the Prophets" really seems to be a shorthand way of referring to the entire Hebrew Scriptures (which also includes the Writings, the third and final division, consisting of books like Psalms and Proverbs). In essence, then, what the Lord is saying here in Matthew 7 is that everything God has spoken to his people, all the various teachings and commands about how to interact with other people, can be summarized in this: "Whatever you want others to do to you, do that to them." God's instruction to us regarding our interactions with other people is that we should always seek to do good for others in the same way we want others to do us good.

Yet elsewhere in the New Testament we read that "the whole law is fulfilled in one word [command]: 'You shall love your neighbor as yourself'" (Gal. 5:14). So, in Galatians, Paul boils the law of God down to one command: "Love your neighbor as yourself." Why the difference from what Jesus says in Matthew 7?

There really is no difference. To do good for your neighbor in the same way that you would like them to do good for you is exactly what it means to love your neighbor as yourself. To love your neighbor as yourself means to joyfully resolve to act for their good.

We know that when the Bible says "neighbor" it refers to all people around us—our coworkers, family members, fellow church members, friends, and the people in our neighborhood and community. This means that we are commanded to love *all* people with this love of joyful resolve. Yet there's still a distinction between

the ways Christians are commanded to love those outside the church and those inside the church.

Loving Those Outside the Church

Toward those outside the church, Christians are commanded to strictly show the love of joyful resolve. By
"strictly," I don't mean that it's wrong to love those outside the church with some affection, but God's command
in this regard doesn't require it. What is strictly required
of Christians is that we joyfully seek the good of all people, even those outside the faith. The clearest example is
the Lord's command to "love your enemies" (Matt. 5:44).

In the early days of my Christian life, I was perplexed
by this command. I sat around at times praying for God
to change my feelings toward those I disliked. *If only that
were to happen,* I thought, *then I could genuinely love my
enemies.* Loving my enemies meant working up affection in my heart toward them (and, of course, praying for
them and wishing them well). But I had misunderstood
what love was, particularly love for one's enemies. Jesus's
command here is, in essence, "Joyfully do good to others,
regardless of how you feel about them." In the case of
your enemies, this means to joyfully do good to those
whom you almost certainly dislike.

It is possible to dislike much of someone's character
(so that you feel repulsed by them) and yet still love them
(joyfully seek to do them good). This is what the Bible
means when it says that "God so loved the world" (John

3:16) but at the same time "his soul hates the wicked" (Ps. 11:5). Love and hate in this regard aren't opposites. God hates the character of the person who habitually disregards him and selfishly seeks his own good at others' expense. Yet at the same time, God gladly seeks to do him good—he loves that wicked person. The greatness of this love is demonstrated by the cost that he is willing to pay to carry it out for those who are his enemies: "God shows his love for us in that while we were still sinners, Christ died for us" (Rom. 5:8).

It's critical for us to grasp this because loving our enemies (or even just those we don't like) is one of the crying needs of the day for Christians in America. On one hand, we are living in a time of ever-increasing polarization between those with differing views on… well, just about everything. Impatience and even outright hatred characterize individual interactions between those with disagreeing opinions. If we want to be salt and light, if we want to show others the way (and the glory!) of Jesus, we must engage with them out of love with a heart that joyfully seeks their good.

On the other hand, we're living in a culture where most everyone publicly applauds niceness, generosity, and charity. Being kind to others, giving to those in need, and fighting for the poor are all good things, of course, and Christians ought to be engaging in them. But a genuine love for one's enemies—not merely mouthing the words but having a robust desire and glad commitment to seek the good of those who hate you—is something so counterintuitive to our culture and to human nature that it stands out like a peacock in a crowd. Loving our enemies displays the glory of God in a way that little else can.

So this is how we are to love those around us who are not Christians. It doesn't matter if the affection is there or not. We are to set about seeing how we might gladly do them good with our prayers, our words, and our actions.[1]

Loving Those Inside the Church

But there's an additional command God gives to us as Christians when it comes to loving those inside the church. While Christians are certainly called to love one another with resolve love, we're also called to love one another with familial affection. We are called to grow in truly *liking* those who are in the church with us.

Paul puts it succinctly in Romans 12:10: "Love one another with brotherly affection." Later, the apostle Peter encourages the church in the same way: "Finally, all of you, have unity of mind, sympathy, brotherly love, a tender heart, and a humble mind" (1 Peter 3:8).

---

1 In the same way that past theologians used the term "complacence" to speak of what I call "affection love," they used the term "benevolence" to describe what I call "resolve love." Here's Edwards again: "Love of benevolence is that affection or propensity of the heart to any being, which causes it to incline to its well-being, or disposes it to desire and take pleasure in its happiness" (Edwards, 1:123). Some readers may prefer to use the terms "complacence" and "benevolence" instead of the terms I've chosen.

Brotherly love or affection is the type of love that family members possess for one another. This is not merely the glad resolve for one another's benefit (as good as that is in and of itself) but also a love that is warmed with affection for one another. I have an older brother and two younger sisters. Whenever I get together with my siblings, no matter how long it's been, the old affection between us quickly springs up again. All the time we've spent together, all the highs and lows, all the laughter and tears, all the forgiveness and encouragement, all the inside jokes and practical jokes, and all the years of being a family together and being committed to loving one another have produced a deep fondness for one another. (Though even now, I can hear one of my siblings quipping, "Speak for yourself, buddy.")

In the same way, the resolve love we possess for one another in the church is to be sweetened with an appreciation and relish for our brothers and sisters in Christ. How is this possible, especially since in the church we find a mishmash of all sorts of people, some completely unlike each other and with very little in common? How can we genuinely have affection for other Christians who are so different from us? It all comes back around to our love for God.

The reality is that Christ dwells in his church and all the individual members of it. Even if we find no natural grounds for affection for others in the church, as we see Christ in them (reflected in their demeanor, words, and

Chapter Four ▪ 47

actions) our hearts will be drawn to him in them. As we spend time together and see the beauty of Christ in one another, we will be drawn to one another in affection.

To recap, then, our love for God is to be the love of affection, of relish and delight. Our love for other people is to be the love of joyful resolve. But for one specific group—fellow Christians—our love is to be resolve love mingled with a growing affection love.

Do you see how this helps us narrow our understanding of discipleship? Now we have specific questions to ask about growing in love as a disciple: How do we grow in our affections, delight, and adoration of God? How do we grow in our joyful resolve to do good for others? And for our fellow Christians, how do we also grow in our affection for them?

But before we attempt to answer these questions, we must ensure that we understand what it means to trust and fear God because we are to be growing in these ways as well. In the next chapter, we'll turn our attention to what it means to trust God.

Chapter Five

What Does It Mean to Trust God?

In our culture, when someone speaks of believing in God or having faith, what they often mean is that they believe that God exists. In the Bible, however, believing in God means trusting in God.

Trust is at the heart of what it means to be a Christian. It's not enough to merely believe that God exists. The Bible makes this evident: "You believe that God is one; you do well. Even the demons believe—and shudder!" (James 2:19). Acknowledging that God exists is good, James says, but it's not nearly enough. Even demons acknowledge his existence—and they shudder because God is their all-powerful enemy. There must be more. James points to the good works a Christian does as evidence that there is something more. But what is this something more?

Chapter Five ▪ 49

It's genuine trust in God. It's entrusting ourselves to Christ, believing that he has the power to save us and that he shows us the mercy of receiving us in our sin, death, and helplessness. It's doing what he says because we trust his wisdom and the love he has for us. From start to finish, the Christian life is about trusting God as he is offered to us in Christ. The trust that Christ will deliver us from the penalty of our sins is the same trust that leads us to obey him out of our confidence in his wisdom, authority, and love for us.

Now, on one hand, when it comes to the specific trust in Jesus to deliver you from your sins and reconcile you to God forever, either you trust him in this way or you don't. If you trust Jesus, you are reconciled to God and completely forgiven of all your sins: "Therefore, since we have been justified by faith, we have peace with God through our Lord Jesus Christ" (Rom. 5:1). If you don't trust him, you are still alienated from God and face the penalty for your sins. In this sense, there are no degrees of trust.

But on the other hand, growing in our trust in God—even after we have trusted in Christ's sacrifice for us—is something we continue to do throughout our lives. It's possible to trust Jesus to save you from your sins but to not trust him fully in every area of your life. In fact, not only is it possible, it's the reality of the Christian life. This is what it means to wrestle with unbelief. We call this "wrestling" because we want to trust

God fully yet struggle to do so. I might worry about whether the money will be there to meet my family's needs this month because I don't fully trust God to keep his promise to provide for all our needs. But the more I grow in my trust and confidence in him, the less I worry.

When we say that one of the key aspects of discipleship is growing in trust in God, this is what we mean. Even after we come to faith in Christ, God desires for us to increasingly trust him through all the trials and circumstances of our lives.

Jesus Trusted God

Jesus understood this and continually demonstrated what it looks like to completely trust in God. If we want to see this clearly in the Scriptures, we need only to look to the garden of Gethsemane, the place of Jesus's greatest testing. Jesus prayed earnestly and fervently for the trial he had to face—bearing the guilt of sin and the wrath of God on the cross—to be taken from him. But ultimately, his prayer was a prayer of trust in his Father. "And going a little farther he fell on his face and prayed, saying, 'My Father, if it be possible, let this cup pass from me; nevertheless, not as I will, but as you will'" (Matt. 26:39).

Facing the greatest trial of his life and understanding the agony of what he would suffer, Jesus prayed that God would somehow take that away from him. He didn't want to undergo the torture. Yet he ultimately set aside his own desires and rested in what his Father deemed best. Jesus trusted God perfectly. To be his disciple means striving for that perfect trust as well.

What We Trust

Before we move on, I think it's helpful for us to ask, "What exactly is it about God that we are called to trust?" When we move on to the question of "How do we grow in our trust?" it will be helpful to have these specifics.

I think we can point to three things we are called to trust, as long as we don't lose sight of the fact that it is "who" we are called to trust rather than "what." That is, our trust is first and foremost in a person (actually, the three persons of the triune God), not in a thing or a set of facts.

First, then, *we trust God's character*. We trust that he always tells us the truth. We trust his benevolence, and particularly his benevolence toward us—that he always desires and is at work for our good. This trust is the antithesis of the distrust that was at the heart of the very first human sin—Adam and Eve's disobedience in the garden of Eden. Eve was tempted to believe that God was withholding something good from her and that he didn't really have her best interests at heart. Because she distrusted him, she ate the fruit he had forbidden her to eat. The fall of humanity means that now, sadly, this distrust naturally resides in the heart of every human being. Even after we come to Christ, even after we are born again, we must fight against this distrust, which remains in our flesh until the day we die. It comes to us in essentially every temptation we face (at least when we aren't sinning out of ignorance).

Whenever we know what God has said about something and yet desire to do otherwise, in that temptation is the whisper, "God doesn't want what's best for you." This is the fight of faith that takes place in our hearts whenever we face difficult circumstances or tragedy. In those times, Satan will always press on our pain and on that natural distrust of God: "God says that he is love? And you believe it? Then how do you make sense of what you're going through? Or maybe he *is* love, but it's clear that he doesn't love *you*." Growing as a disciple means growing in trust in God throughout our lives—our trust that he is straightforward in what he says to us, transparent in his intentions toward us, and unwaveringly committed to us in his love.

Second, *we trust all the truths God has spoken.* This is a trust that rests on our confidence that God completely knows reality and never lies. Thus, whatever God has spoken in his Word can be completely relied on as true, and we are to stake our lives on it.

For example, take the biblical truth that God is sovereign, that he rules over all the earth and nothing happens that is out of his control. He either decrees or permits all that takes place. This is a fine-sounding theological statement to hear and affirm in an easy

Chapter Five ▪ 53

chair, but having firsthand experience with the depths of grief or evil in the world makes this statement much more difficult to believe. If God had not articulated this truth to us in his Word, we would likely doubt whether it was true based on what we see and experience. But it is true, and God calls us to trust that it is true and to live our lives accordingly.

Another example of one of these truths and how our trust in it works out is in Isaiah 2:22, where the prophet speaks God's word to the people: "Stop regarding man in whose nostrils is breath, for of what account is he?"

We naturally tend to think that what others think of us matters a lot. We want other people to think highly of us. We want to be held in high regard—it's the appeal of being famous. *If many others know me and love me, then that validates me as great and good.* But even if we don't have a strong desire to become famous, we at least don't want others to be upset with us. And heaven forbid that someone dislikes us.

But God says that man is of little regard. We tend to have an exaggerated sense of our own importance. But in the ultimate scheme of things, the judgment of other human beings is of very little weight. It is the judgment of God that matters; it's what he thinks of you that counts for everything.

Growing in trust that this is true, then, means we should become less and less concerned about what others think of us or say about us because we know that what we are doing is good and right. Growing in our trust of the truths of God's Word means seeing the world rightly so we can live accordingly.

Third, *we trust all the promises God has made.* In my experience, there is a tendency among Christians to *look back* to what Jesus did to save us and then *look forward* in confidence that we will go to heaven when we die. Both are glorious and good, of course. But what isn't good is what this often means as we *look around* at our present circumstances. We're filled with anxiety because we fail to recognize that God is at work in the present too. I have confidence that God has saved me, and I have confidence that God will receive me when I die, but where do I find the confidence to face all my present trials and circumstances? The answer is in the promises of God.

God has given us specific promises for a myriad of situations and temptations that we face here and now. His aim is for us to trust in those promises so we can have joy and peace and overcome sin as we grow in Christlike character and purity. This is what Peter writes about in 2 Peter 1:3–4:

> His divine power has granted to us all things that pertain to life and godliness, through the knowledge of him who called us to his own glory and excellence, by which he has granted to us his precious and very great promises, so that through them you may become partakers of the

Chapter Five ▪ 55

divine nature, having escaped from the corruption that is in the world because of sinful desire.

It is through God's precious and very great promises
that we become partakers of the divine nature—that
is, partakers in the character of God. Believing God's
promises sanctifies us and makes us more like Christ.

I'll give just one example. Our culture is largely un-
familiar with the sin of covetousness (that is, it's not
recognized as a sin at all), even though it is one of the
Ten Commandments. "You shall not covet your neighbor's house; you shall not covet your neighbor's wife, or
his male servant, or his female servant, or his ox, or his
donkey, or anything that is your neighbor's" (Ex. 20:17).
Here God forbids us from looking at what someone
else has and desiring it in our hearts so much that we
wish it were ours instead of theirs. How does one overcome that natural human temptation? By trusting in
God's promise.

In Psalm 84:11, we read this promise about God:
"For the LORD God is a sun and shield; the LORD
will give grace and glory; no good thing will He withhold from those who walk uprightly" (NKJV). When
we are tempted to covet, we think, "That is something
good that I can't have... but I want it." But this also
says something about God, doesn't it? It says, "God is
withholding something good from me." The promise
of Psalm 84 tells us a different story, though. *No good*

56 ■ *A Simple Model of Discipleship*

thing does God withhold from those who walk uprightly. If I trust in Christ and follow him, there is *nothing* good that God will withhold from me. As Christians, we are tempted to think, "If I had that house, I would be happier and better off," or "If I had a child like him who was so well behaved, I would be happier and better off." But it's not true. "Better off" doesn't mean a carefree life. If you are a Christian, there are problematic people in your life whom God is using to make you more like Christ, which will ultimately make you *better off.* The point is, as you believe this promise from God, the nerve that causes you to feel the temptation to covet is severed and you become more like Christ in your trust in God.[1]

Which Promises Are for Us?

One final question before we move on: How do we know which promises are for us? More specifically, we might say, "God gave many promises to the people of Israel in the Old Testament, and he sometimes gave promises to specific individuals. But which of those promises still pertain to Christians today?"

Let's look to one New Testament passage for help. In Hebrews 13:5, the author of the letter, quoting from

---

1 While one might exist, I know of no better book about how God's promises help us overcome temptation than John Piper's *Future Grace* (Multnomah, 1995) or the helpful abridged version of that book titled *Battling Unbelief* (Multnomah, 2007), which contains chapters that apply particular promises of God to specific temptations we face.

Joshua 1:5, illustrates how an Old Testament promise to God's people could be applied to New Testament believers: "Keep your life free from love of money, and be content with what you have, for he has said, 'I will never leave you nor forsake you.'"

Interestingly, the original promise from God to Joshua was a specific promise that he would always be with and support Joshua as he led the people of Israel to conquer the land of Canaan. Yet the writer of Hebrews takes that promise and applies it to the lives of all Christians. "Don't let the love of money consume your hearts, but be content with what you have, because God promises that he will always be with you and care for you."

While not every promise made in the Old Testament applies to Christians today (e.g., God's promise to make for David a great name in 1 Chronicles 17:8), and thus there is obviously a need for discernment, we can be confident that any promise God has made to his people as a whole or to one of his children in particular about his protection, provision, love, or care is a promise for us as well.

Charles Spurgeon puts it beautifully:

No promise is of private interpretation. Whatever God has said to any one saint, he has said to all. When he opens a well for one, it is that all may drink. When he openeth a granary-door to

58 ▪ *A Simple Model of Discipleship*

give out food, there may be some one starving man who is the occasion of its being opened, but all hungry saints may come and feed too. Whether He gave the word to Abraham or to Moses, matters not, O believer; He has given it to thee as one of the covenanted seed. There is not a high blessing too lofty for thee, nor a wide mercy too extensive for thee. Lift up now thine eyes to the north and to the south, to the east and to the west, for all this is thine. Climb to Pisgah's top, and view the utmost limit of the divine promise, for the land is all thine own.[2]

As we grow in our trust in God—his character, the truths he's spoken, his promises—we grow as disciples. Now let's move on to what it means to grow as a disciple through fearing God.

---

2 Charles H. Spurgeon, *Morning and Evening*, morning entry for February 23, Bible Gateway, accessed November 5, 2020, https://www.biblegateway.com/devotionals/morning-and-evening/2020/02/23.

Chapter Six

What Does It Mean to Fear God?

The "fear of the Lord" is one of the more perplexing concepts for us as Christians in the West in the twenty-first century. How can you fear God and love him at the same time? It seems you must choose one or the other. Either God is a being of tremendous holiness and wrath and so is preeminently to be feared, or God is a being of immense love, compassion, and tenderness, and thus he is to be loved.

But the problem is—as one quickly realizes when reading the Bible for any length of time—that the Lord is to be feared *and* loved.

> And now, Israel, what does the LORD your God require of you, but to *fear* the LORD your God, to walk in all his ways, to *love* him, to serve the LORD your God with all your

heart and with all your soul, and to keep the commandments and statutes of the LORD, which I am commanding you today for your good? (Deut. 10:12–13, italics added)

Since being a disciple means following Jesus, let's start with this point: Jesus feared God. While there is no place in the Gospels that directly says, "Jesus feared God," Jesus did imply that fearing God was a positive thing. In Luke 18, he told a parable of an unjust judge who was negatively characterized by the fact that he did not fear God. Jesus also directly commanded his disciples to fear God instead of fearing people who might harm them (Luke 12:4–7).

Even if this weren't enough in and of itself to convince us that Jesus himself feared God, there is a rich passage from the Old Testament about the coming Messiah that makes clear that the fear of the Lord is one of his primary attributes. This is Isaiah 11:1–3:

There shall come forth a shoot from the stump of Jesse,
and a branch from his roots shall bear fruit.
And the Spirit of the LORD shall rest upon him,
the Spirit of wisdom and understanding,
the Spirit of counsel and might,
the Spirit of knowledge and the fear of the LORD.
And his delight shall be in the fear of the LORD.

The Spirit of the Lord will rest on the Messiah, and it would be characteristic of the Messiah that he would fear the Lord. But not only did Jesus as the Messiah fear the Lord, he also *delighted* in that fear. But what kind of fear can be delighted in?

The Fear of the Lord

The fear of the Lord is not "fear" in the common, contemporary way we use the term. When we use the word "fear," we're almost always speaking of the emotion that results from a sense that something bad is going to happen to us. That fear may range from a mild concern to an overwhelming sense of dread, but at the heart of the fear is the sense that we are going to experience something harmful to us.

When I was about eight years old, I discovered I had a paralyzing fear of heights. I was climbing the stairs of the Eiffel Tower replica at a local amusement park, and the stairs were made of metal grates so you were able to see through them. I remember looking down and my legs instantly turning to stone. I was terrified that I was going to fall. The amusing thing is that I was only about two and a half stories off the ground at the time. (Perhaps even more amusing is that even though I've been back to that amusement park numerous times, I've never found a reason to go back up those stairs.) When we fear something, that fear leads us to avoid it as much as possible.

But a passage from the book of Exodus helps us see there are different ways that the word "fear" was used in the Old Testament. Immediately after the Lord gave Moses the Ten Commandments, this is what followed in Exodus 20:18–20:

> Now when all the people saw the thunder and the flashes of lightning and the sound of the trumpet and the mountain smoking, the people were afraid and trembled, and they stood far off and said to Moses, "You speak to us, and we will listen; but do not let God speak to us, lest we die." Moses said to the people, "Do not fear, for God has come to test you, that the fear of him may be before you, that you may not sin."

Note verse 20, which essentially says, "Don't fear—God has come to test you so that you may fear him." Obviously, then, there are two different kinds of fear. There must be, because otherwise what Moses says makes no sense; it would be a contradiction. (By the way, both the verb "to fear" and the noun "fear" are from the same Hebrew root. These are not two completely different Hebrew terms for "fear.") One fear here is to be shunned, and one to be embraced.

It seems clear that the fear we should shun is our contemporary sense of the word. It is simply to be afraid of

Chapter Six ▪ 63

God. Moses is saying to the people, "Don't dread—God has not come to hurt you. Instead, God has come to you for your good. He has come that you might *fear* him (in another sense of the word)." Again, it makes no sense to think that this second sense of the word "fear" can mean the same as the first. Otherwise, Moses is saying, "Don't be afraid of God. He has come to test you so that you would be afraid of him." So, this second fear must be a different kind of fear. But what kind?

Fear as Reverence

The fear of the Lord is *rightly reverencing God as God.* Of course, "reverence" isn't a word that we commonly use in our twenty-first-century society. To put it a little differently, then, the fear of the Lord is a deep respect full of awe and wonder for God. We'll unpack this shortly, but first I want to emphasize that this reverencing fear contains no trace of the fear that God is going to hurt us.

There is indeed a situation in which human beings should rightly be terrified of God. It's when we stand guilty before God because of the evil we have done. The Bible is clear that all human beings have broken God's law. We are legally guilty before God and face punishment for that guilt. The Bible is also clear that the evil of our sins makes God justly angry, so we face a righteously angry God who knows all our sins and who is committed to punishing all evil in the universe. To seriously consider standing before an angry, all-powerful, all-knowing God who is a righteous Judge is indeed a terrifying reality.

But when we genuinely come to trust in Christ, all that changes. The Bible assures us, "There is therefore now no condemnation for those who are in Christ Jesus" (Rom. 8:1). The word "condemnation" is specifically used as a legal term. It means to be declared guilty in a court of law, as we once were before God. But now, because Christ died in your place, you are no longer guilty, and you no longer face any punishment. Praise God for his mercy!

The Bible also says that, for those who trust in Christ, Jesus is "the propitiation for our sins" (1 John 2:2). A "propitiation" is a sacrifice that turns away God's wrath. By his death, Jesus bore all God's anger that was directed at you because of your sins. That anger is completely exhausted now—God is not angry at you anymore.

As Christians, therefore, we should never be terrified that God is going to punish us. Will he discipline us? Yes. Will he punish us? No. That's not just playing word games—there is a world of difference between those two words and between the experiences of the Christian who understands them rightly and the one who doesn't. When the state punishes a criminal, it is seeking to exact retribution for the crime committed. In other words, punishment means you are paying for the wrongs you have done. But Christ bore our

Chapter Six ▪ 65

punishment in his body on the cross (1 Peter 2:24). Don't you see? If you are in Christ, that means that in his death, Jesus took all the *punishment* you deserve. You will never have to pay the penalty for your sins. Jesus paid it all for you.

Discipline is a completely different matter. When a father (rightly and sincerely) disciplines his child, he's not exacting payment for the wrongs the child has done. Instead, he's bringing painful consequences into the child's life to steer him away from wrong and harm and toward what is right and good for him (and others). The judge punishes the criminal out of a right regard for justice. The father disciplines the child out of love. This is reason to praise God too. If we are in Christ, God is our Father and loves us enough to correct us. This is Hebrews 12:5–6 (quoting from Prov. 3:11–12):

> My son, do not regard lightly the discipline of the Lord,
> nor be weary when reproved by him.
> For the Lord disciplines the one he loves,
> and chastises every son whom he receives.

Being disciplined is not a particularly pleasant experience. And it's certainly possible to say that we "fear" discipline. No child wants a spanking, because it does hurt some. No one likes the aspect of correction that humbles us. But this fear doesn't qualify as fear that is afraid of God because he is going to hurt us. The situation is similar to facing surgery. We wouldn't fear the surgeon who was going to operate on us even though we might rightly fear the pain of the surgery.

The fear of the Lord is free from the fear of God hurting us.

How the Fear of God Looks in Our Lives

So, to grow in the fear of the Lord, then, means to grow deeper in our reverence for God. To provide a little more context for what this looks like, it seems that the Bible speaks of the fear of the Lord working out in our lives in several different ways. One who fears God (1) trembles at God's majesty and greatness, (2) recognizes and gladly submits to his authority, and (3) detests all that stands contrary to God (that is, all that is evil).

To Reverence God as God Means to Tremble at His Majesty and Holiness

Psalm 96:1–9 makes this connection clear (italics added):

> Oh sing to the LORD a new song;
> sing to the LORD, all the earth!
> Sing to the LORD, bless his name;
> tell of his salvation from day to day.
> Declare his glory among the nations,
> his marvelous works among all the peoples!

For great is the LORD, and greatly to be praised;
he is to be *feared* above all gods.
For all the gods of the peoples are worthless idols,
but the LORD made the heavens.
Splendor and *majesty* are before him;
strength and beauty are in his sanctuary.
Ascribe to the LORD, O families of the peoples,
ascribe to the LORD glory and strength!
Ascribe to the LORD the glory due his name;
bring an offering, and come into his courts!
Worship the LORD in the splendor of holiness;
tremble before him, all the earth!

To fear God here means to consider and see the splendor, majesty, and holiness of God and to tremble at his greatness. Fearing God in this regard is in direct contrast with the indifference toward him we so often feel as fallen human beings. But who, seeing God rightly, would not tremble!

To Reverence God as God Means to Recognize and Gladly Submit to His Authority

Psalm 112:1 speaks to the fear of the Lord manifesting itself in gladly bowing our knee to God's authority: "Blessed is the man who fears the LORD, who greatly delights in his commandments!" Even if fearing the Lord isn't to be equated only with delighting in the Lord's commandments, here those things are synonymous. Hebrew poetry is characterized by parallelism, and here the same idea is stated in different ways. Fearing the Lord equals greatly delighting in God's commandments.

What a strange "fear" that is full of joy in commandments! Yet this is the fear of the Lord. The one who fears God rejoices in his commandments and is certain they are good and right and true. He has a deep reverence for God's authority to command what he will. And he has a deep reverence for God's wisdom to know and to command what is good.

To Reverence God as God Means to Hate What Is Evil

More than anything, the bulk of the Bible's references to the fear of the Lord are about how it leads a person to abhor what is evil and, therefore, to refrain from engaging in it. This is presumably because engaging in evil is a great dishonor to God. It is what's behind Joseph's fear of the Lord when his master's wife tries to seduce him: "How then can I do this great wickedness and sin against God?" (Gen. 39:9).

Looking at the fear of God from the opposite perspective (from the one who has no fear of him at all), we see that the appeal of evil keeps the wicked from fearing God. Psalm 36:1–4 paints a disquieting picture of the wicked person in his contemplation:

Transgression speaks to the wicked deep in his heart;
there is no fear of God before his eyes.

Chapter Six ▪ 69

For he flatters himself in his own eyes
that his iniquity cannot be found out and hated.
The words of his mouth are trouble and deceit;
he has ceased to act wisely and do good.
He plots trouble while on his bed;
he sets himself in a way that is not good;
he does not reject evil.

Transgression allures the wicked person deep in his heart, so he does not reject evil. This leads to the ultimate pronouncement that "there is no fear of God before his eyes."

Proverbs 8:13 states it forthrightly: "The fear of the LORD is hatred of evil." When we have a deep reverence for God, we love what he loves and hate what he hates. We especially hate anything that would dishonor him. A fear of God and a love for what is evil are like the repelling poles of a magnet—they simply cannot be found together.

To the degree that we are growing in recognizing and consequently standing in awe of God, to the degree that we are growing in acknowledging and gladly submitting to his authority, and to the degree that we are growing in our hatred for evil, we are growing in the fear of the Lord.

Chapter Seven

What About Growing in the Knowledge of God?

When I was a child, I wanted to know everything. I loved books, and I had interests that ranged from the lives of the presidents to the stories of Ancient Egypt to the characteristics of every animal under the sun. My mom has often said that the only day she could count on peace in the car on the ride home from school was the day my monthly Scholastic order came in and I was too engrossed in my books to pick fights with my sisters. It's no surprise that one of my childhood heroes was Encyclopedia Brown, the boy detective who never met a mystery he couldn't solve thanks to his wit and his encyclopedic knowledge of... well, everything.

When I became a Christian in my mid-twenties, it was only to be expected that I should be in awe of those with extensive knowledge of the facts of the Bible. The masters of Bible trivia surely had to be, in my mind, the great saints of the faith. If someone had said to me, "Learning the Bible is what it means to grow as a disciple," I think I would have readily agreed.

Perhaps you would, as well. But consider further. Does learning the Bible always equate to growth in discipleship? No, it doesn't. I'm not insinuating (obviously, I hope) that it's a bad thing to know the Bible inside and out. But I'm saying that it can become a bad thing if it's done solely to make you a master of Bible facts. You can memorize a tremendous number of facts from the Bible and still not comprehend its meaning. That's not good. At all. In fact, it has the makings of a very dangerous combination of pride and ignorance—and it certainly doesn't mean you're growing as a disciple of Jesus.

But even understanding the meaning of the Bible, over and above all the facts, doesn't equate to being a mature disciple either. It's true that as we genuinely grow as disciples, we will grow in our understanding of the Bible, but the reverse of that equation doesn't always hold. Sadly, it's quite possible for us to learn the meaning of more and more passages and books of the Bible and yet not advance a step toward greater godliness. See exhibit A—the Pharisees in the Gospel accounts. The Pharisees knew their Scriptures better than anyone else in Jesus's day, yet they still didn't know God. It's quite possible that there are many people today who know their Bible thoroughly and are still self-righteous prigs whose hearts have no real love for God or others.

I bring this up here because of the drive I see among devoted American Christians to study the Bible for the sake of intellectually comprehending its meaning. The underlying assumption, it seems to me, is that when we obtain this understanding, we will be mature and will have grown as disciples. It's almost as if we think that understanding the Bible is the be-all and end-all of the Christian life.

But this knowledge, this understanding, is never an end in itself. It's worth saying that again: *understanding the meaning of what God has spoken to us is never an end in and of itself.* God's Word always calls for a response from us. Our growth and maturity as disciples lies in that response. We can continue to stuff our minds full of fact after fact about God and the Scriptures, but until we respond to what we know in love, trust, and fear, we aren't growing more like Christ.

But Knowledge Must Come First

So, knowledge of the Bible isn't enough. But this doesn't mean that knowledge isn't important. Knowledge must come first. The knowledge of God and his Word is a precursor to loving, trusting, and fearing him. In fact, one of the most important things for us

Chapter Seven ▪ 73

to remember as we think about growing as disciples is that love (affection love), trust, and fear are always a response. We never suddenly begin to feel affection love out of nowhere. Our love is always a response to someone or something. The same is true of our trust and our fear—they are responses.

If we don't truly know God, we won't respond to him rightly in love, trust, and fear. The way we come to know him is through understanding what he has revealed to us and most clearly and significantly through what he has spoken to us in the Bible. To grow as a disciple, we *must* know and understand it.

So even though I won't be talking further about how to study the Bible to understand it, it's not because that's unimportant. Rather, it's because it is outside the scope of this book to talk about the best ways to go about understanding and interpreting the Bible. What I will say emphatically before I turn from the subject, though, is that we must make every effort to grow in our understanding of the Bible. We should study it ourselves and seek out teachers who can explain it more clearly to us. We should pray earnestly for understanding (Ps. 119) and strive for it. I'm assuming that all that is a given and you recognize those things as important components for progressing as a disciple. But let's also make sure that understanding isn't seen as the end of discipleship but rather as a means to love, trust, and fear God (and, likewise, to

74 ▪ A Simple Model of Discipleship

love other people). Let's press on then, by the grace of God and with the help of the Spirit, to do just that.[1]

Two Types of Knowledge

There's something else that needs to be said about knowledge—something particularly important to the dynamics of how knowledge relates to loving, trusting, and fearing God.

First, a short definition of knowledge. What does it mean to have knowledge? Knowledge is an awareness of something that is true, an accurate perception of a certain aspect of reality. This short definition helps to see a little more clearly what we need to understand next—there is more than one type of knowledge, more than one way to know something about reality.

I can know that a wasp's sting is painful in a couple of different ways. I can know by reading a scientific journal, with the explanation of how it affects the nerves in our skin (the preferred knowledge). Or I can know it by inadvertently putting my hand near a nest and getting stung by a wasp (not preferred but,

---

1 This seems to be a good point to share why I included this chapter about knowledge, especially since it breaks the logical chain of the chapters before and after it. First, when it comes to the topic of Christian discipleship, it seems absurd not to say anything about the significance of the knowledge that comes to us through God's Word. Second, as I will detail shortly, right knowledge is foundational to rightly loving, trusting, and fearing God. I think it's important to discuss why and how different types of knowledge affect our growth in love, trust, and fear before turning our attention to the question of *how* we grow in love, trust, and fear.

unfortunately, the firsthand knowledge I obtained a couple of summers ago).

This illustration helps us to see that there are two types of knowledge: (1) knowledge comprehended by the mind and (2) knowledge conveyed by the senses.

Knowledge Comprehended by the Mind

Knowledge comprehended by the mind is an understanding of the facts. This knowledge might come through understanding written or spoken words (e.g., an article that conveys the fact that tree frogs are an endangered species). Or it might come through experience (e.g., I know a friend is kind because of the repeated acts of compassion I've seen them carry out). I suppose one could also argue that it can come through intuition (e.g., I know in my gut he's not being truthful), though there is some question of how much of that is a judgment based on past experience.

Here's where this comes into play in our spiritual lives and discipleship:

- I can know truth about God by understanding his Word.[2] (e.g., God is holy. God never lies. God is just.)

---

2   Since God is the ultimate author of the Bible, when we understand the meaning intended by a biblical author in a certain passage, we understand the meaning intended by God.

- I can know truth about God by recognizing what he has done in my life. (e.g., God loves to give good gifts. God gives generously. God is faithful to his promises. God answers prayer.)

This is the first type of knowledge—that which comes through our reason and is comprehended through the mind.

Knowledge Conveyed by the Senses

But there is also a second type of knowledge, an awareness of reality which we can gain only through our senses. I know the tart sweetness of grapes because I've tasted them. I know the smoothness of silk because I've felt it. I know the sulfurous odor of rotten eggs because I've smelled them. I know how urgent and alarming a cry of pain sounds because I've heard one. I really and truly know these things in a way that I couldn't know them through a description from someone else. Words can't convey this knowledge to the mind, it must come through the experience of our senses.

At first blush, we're tempted to ask, "How does the knowledge that comes through our senses have anything to do with our relationship with God? After all, we don't experience him with our senses." With our physical senses, no. But our souls have a sense as well— the ability to "taste" that which is glorious, good, beautiful, and awe-inspiring. We might even say that what the soul tastes is "glory"—the excellence or beauty of someone or something.

It's our souls' ability to "taste" that results in being moved to tears when we come to a profound moment in a book or movie, like the stunning moment of sacrificial love and grace in *Les Misérables* when the Bishop of Digne gives his silver candlesticks to the thief Jean Valjean (who had stolen all his other silver) so that he may go free and have a second chance at life. We are moved as we taste this beauty—as is Valjean, whose life is transformed.

Experiencing the glory of God, the bright excellence of his greatness and goodness, is conveyed to us (in this life) through our souls' ability to taste. This indeed is what the psalmist means when he encourages us to "*taste* and see that the LORD is good!" (Ps. 34:8, italics added). Unfortunately, being fallen human beings means our souls' "palates" don't function completely accurately. There are many things that taste good to us that are actually evil. In our corrupt state, we don't have the ability to truly discern who God is when our souls get a taste of his glory—as if we were to get a taste of a delicious, homemade birthday cake and mistakenly identify it as a Twinkie. But in conversion, God gives us the ability to taste rightly. He gives us this knowledge, a true taste of his glory, in a way that changes us forever and leaves us longing to taste more.

This is exactly how the apostle Paul describes the moment of regeneration in 2 Corinthians 4:6: "For

78 ▪ A Simple Model of Discipleship

God, who said, 'Let light shine out of darkness,' has shone in our hearts to give the light of the knowledge of the glory of God in the face of Jesus Christ."[3]

Which Knowledge Really Matters?

So, there is the knowledge of God which comes through our minds, and the knowledge of God which comes through our senses. We can truly know God when we understand what he has spoken about himself and when we experience him by tasting his glory. We can read that God is holy and understand this means he is completely free from all evil and stands in utter opposition to it. That is indeed true and right knowledge. But it's a completely different kind of knowledge to be aware that this God is a living, personal being and that you are standing before him in your moral impurity (like the experience of Isaiah the prophet recorded in Isaiah 6). It's moving from knowledge as an intellectual concept to knowledge through a sensory experience.

Our knee-jerk reaction might be to think that only this second type of knowledge really matters. But that's not right—both types of knowledge are important. Without intellectual knowledge of God, we would assuredly misinterpret our experience of God. Without

---

3   "Regeneration" is another term for being "born again" (John 3:3). Regeneration is a resetting of the taste buds of our soul's palate, giving us a taste for God and all that is good. Sanctification is a retraining of that palate to "hate what is evil and love what is good."

the plainly stated truth in God's Word of his love for us, our circumstances at times would undoubtedly lead us to be in bald terror of him. Even with the stated assurance of his love in his Word, we find ourselves tempted to servile fear at times. How much more so would we without it? But without the knowledge conveyed through our soul's taste of his glory, there can be no real heart relationship with God—only dry, sterile information cataloged in the archives of our minds. In this case, God is no different from a historical figure we learn about in books. So we shouldn't think we can dispose of one type of knowledge or the other.

Both head knowledge and sense knowledge are necessary, and both are helpful for growing in our love, trust, and fear of God. In fact, they very often work together, particularly when it comes to tasting God's glory. This sense knowledge often comes *through* our head knowledge, our understanding of God through what he has revealed in the Bible.

With all that being said, it is this second type of knowledge—the knowledge of sensory experience—that matters most when it comes to changing us. Sensory knowledge is the most effective at arousing our loves, hates, fears, and longings. This is the type of knowledge that moves us in the sense of evoking a response. A bee sting on the foot is much more effective at getting a child to wear shoes in the summer than any parental warning about bee stings could ever be.

And one taste of a dish that looks unappetizing but is actually delicious prompts a child to eat her dinner far more readily than any parent's description of its culinary virtues ever could.

This is true in our relationship with God as well. The more we "taste and see" the glory of the Lord's goodness, the more we will love him. The more we taste and see the glory of his faithfulness, the more we will trust him. The more we taste and see the glory of his holiness and majesty, the more we will fear him.

The problem, however, is that really and profoundly tasting God's glory is not something we have control over. In this case, we are like the gardener who can till the ground, plant the seeds, and root out the weeds, but only God can give the sunshine and rain that makes the garden grow. In the same way, we can understand a magnificent truth about God from the Bible, but only the Spirit can enable us to truly taste it as magnificent and to see God as magnificent in light of that truth.

Again, though, if we are Christians, it's important to remember that we have already experienced this "glory" knowledge. (If you are not a Christian, a good prayer to pray is "God, please show me your glory in Jesus! Help me to truly see him for who he is." God loves to do this—sincerely ask him and see!) We have tasted the glory of the Lord. To move forward in Christlikeness, then—in love, trust, and fear of God—we need to taste it again and again.

Chapter Seven ▪ 81

Let's press on and consider the specific ways we can till the ground, plant the seeds, and clear the weeds for the Spirit to do this work only he can do—giving us a taste of the glory of God, his truth, and his world.

Chapter Eight

How Do We Grow in Love for God?

Love is like water. But affection love is like a fire. Just as every fire starts with a spark of some sort, affection love always starts with a moment of pleasure when we enjoy something or find someone beautiful or good. This first spark is not yet love—we may not even be consciously aware of it—but affection love always starts with it. But what fans this spark of pleasure into the flame of love?

That's the question I want to address first. Before we talk about how we grow in love for God specifically, it's helpful to consider how affection love grows generally. So how does the flicker of a flame of affection love grow into a fire? I think there are three ways.

The first way is the most dramatic. It's what happens when a spark meets lighter fluid—the spark flames up into a raging fire immediately. This is what

Chapter Eight ▪ 83

I call a "moment of glory," when you are powerfully struck by beauty or goodness and nearly overwhelmed by the love you feel. The perfect example of this is love at first sight. Boy sees girl and is instantly smitten by her beauty (complete with the sounds of the angelic choir in the background).

These moments of glory are moments we all desire to be caught up in. We'd love to always experience the roaring delight of the pleasure of our loves. But these moments only happen rarely, and they don't last long (no more than you can keep a fire burning on lighter fluid alone). While these moments are wonderful, and while they do help further our love and keep it kindled, we will be frustrated if they are the only experiences of love we have in our lives. They happen too infrequently to satisfy us. But this isn't the only way we experience and grow in affection love.

The second and most common way that affection love grows is by experiencing a particular pleasure repeatedly. What starts as something I enjoyed becomes something I love because I've enjoyed it time and time again. How did you come to love your mom's meatloaf and mashed potatoes so much? It likely isn't because you experienced a moment of profound glory the first time you ate them. You probably don't even remember the first time you ate them. Rather, you love them because you've enjoyed them so many times.

Experiencing love in this way, while not as profound and soul-grabbing as a moment of glory, is still rich and good and desirable. Thinking again of affection love as a fire, this experience is like what happens when we add a log to a fire that is burning nicely. While this experience of affection love isn't as dramatic (sudden) or as hot (overwhelming) as when the fire flames up, the heat is still enjoyable, and it's more sustainable as well.

But there's a third way affection love grows. It's the most mysterious way of all. It grows slowly but with such stealth we don't even see it coming. Then one day, we look around and find ourselves shocked to see it there. This is when we find that we love something after a long force of habit—a habit we didn't even find ourselves really enjoying. Perhaps it was even a habit we disliked. Yet after some length of time of engaging in this habit, we woke to the surprising realization that we actually loved what we were doing or experiencing.

My first memory of making coffee is from my college years. My roommates and I had a little four-cup coffee maker. One night, facing a lengthy study session, I pulled it out and stuck a coffee filter in it. Figuring the filter was the size that it was for a reason, I filled it to the very top with coffee grounds. When the coffee was brewed, it was, as best as I can describe it, utterly heinous. The single sip I took was the only one I could handle. The remainder of the pot went summarily down the drain.

Chapter Eight ▪ 85

A year or so later, though, early one morning in a fog of grogginess, I staggered into the campus Burger King for a cup of coffee with sugar and cream. I wouldn't say it was good, but I was able to manage it. Slowly and surely, though, that hit of caffeine became a habit. Before long, I wasn't merely enduring the taste of the coffee—I was enjoying it. Through the years, that taste became so enjoyable that I gradually started to drink coffee first without sugar, and then eventually even without cream. Via the long, slow road of habit, I had come to love a taste that I at first loathed.

We can think of this third way like when we pile kindling onto a little fire that's just been started. The kindling completely covers up the spark so that you're not even able to see a flame underneath. You're just adding one little stick to another, and then suddenly you look and, lo and behold, there's a rollicking flame.

Affection love either flares up in a moment of glory, burns deeper as we experience pleasure again and again, or appears in our lives mysteriously through our habits. But there's one more aspect of affection love that's like a fire too. Like a fire, if affection love is neglected, it will eventually cool and even go out. And just like the ways a fire can be actively smothered or dampened, there are things we can do (or fail to do) in our lives that will "put out" the affection love we feel for others.

Growing in Our Love for God

What's the spark that starts our love for God? It's the joy that comes from truly grasping his love for us in Christ for the first time. It's a supernatural spark dropped into our dry hearts by the Spirit of God as we hear the message of the good news of Jesus and are born again. From this spark, the fire of our love for God grows. And it grows in all three of the ways that were discussed earlier—in moments of glory, in repeated pleasures, and slowly and stealthily through our habits.

While I want to explain each of these a bit further, I'm shifting my focus here from explanation to application. Recognizing how affection love grows, I want to answer the question, "What do we need to do to help fuel the fire of our love for God?" My answers are not going to be exhaustive, and I suspect some of you will be disappointed that they aren't more specifically practical. Part of the reason for that is the brevity of this book (which I hope will encourage people to actually read it), but another part is that the nature of growing in our love for God isn't tailored to a narrow, one-size-fits-all approach. There are principles, yes, but we all need to work out the specific details in our own unique lives, families, and churches. What I've tried to do below is to articulate the principles for growing in a way that's narrow enough to be helpful for you.

Moments of Glory

First, then, we experience moments of glory when we are dazzled by God's love, goodness, and beauty. Just a few weeks ago, as fall arrived in full here in Virginia, I glanced over at a residential street and was struck by beauty. There was a row of trees along the road right in front of a church, and the trees' leaves were a glowing, neon orange-red. It was truly breathtaking. I experienced a moment of glory as I marveled at the beauty of God reflected in what he had created, causing an intense love for him to surge up in my heart.

Most Christians can recall at least one moment when they have been overwhelmed by God's greatness, goodness, or love. Perhaps for you it was when you first put your trust in Christ, as you realized the gravity of your sins but also the fact that Jesus bore them all. Others might recall how a particular truth proclaimed by their pastor or a verse from a congregational hymn moved them profoundly. Or it might have happened in a way that didn't start with a sermon or a song. The nineteenth-century evangelist D. L. Moody was walking down Wall Street in New York City when he felt the Spirit of God prompt him to find a place to pray to God alone. He immediately did so and later spoke of the profound moment of glory he experienced:

> Ah, what a day!—I cannot describe it, I seldom refer to it, it is almost too sacred an experience

to name—Paul had an experience of which he never spoke for fourteen years—I can only say God revealed Himself to me, and I had such an experience of His love that I had to ask Him to stay His hand.[1]

What can we do to help produce these moments of glory? I'm sorry to be so disappointingly blunt, but the answer is… nothing. These moments of glory that result in flaming love for God will happen throughout our lives as Christians, but there's nothing we can do to prompt a flaming up of affection love in our hearts for God that is this strong. One thing we can do is put ourselves in the "places" where this might happen, but we can't make them happen.[2] These moments are simply gifts from God, and we should gladly receive them as such when they come.

Repeated Pleasures

But it's a different story when it comes to the second way of growing love for God. There are particular ways we can enjoy God's goodness and beauty over and over, and we should strive to fill our lives with these practices.

---

1   Lyle W. Dorsett, *A Passion for Souls: The Life of D. L. Moody* (Chicago: Moody, 1997), 156.

2   I consider those "places" to be in reading and meditating on the Bible, in prayer, in worshiping together with others, and in nature.

Chapter Eight ▪ 89

Recalling again that affection love is a response to God, here are those practices:

Savor God's Beauty and Glory Again and Again

My grandmother's living room is decorated differently than most people's. Covering one huge wall, where most of us would hang a few pieces of framed art, she has a lifetime of photographs. From her parents to her brother to her husband to her children, grandchildren, and great-grandchildren, we're all there. As she's gotten older, one of her constant refrains has been, "God has been so good to me. My life has been so rich." I can't help but believe that her joy is due in some significant way to those pictures continuously reminding her of those she loves so much. She especially loves to look at pictures of her husband, who died over thirty years ago but with whom she is still enamored and can't wait to see again. She looks at his picture and remembers, "He's the most handsome man I've ever seen." Seeing him reminds her of how much she loves him and stirs that love up again and again. The same is true for us whenever we "see" God's beauty and glory.

While there's not only one way of doing this, one of the primary ways is seeing God where he has most clearly revealed himself—the Bible. I daresay this is what we should primarily seek as we read and meditate on the Bible. Yes, there are commands in the Bible to heed, examples to learn from, and principles for wise living to consider. But first and foremost, we should open our Bible—the self-revelation of God—to learn who he is. Once we have learned, we should open it again and again to "see" him and be reminded of his beauty, goodness, wisdom, and grace. This is what God himself teaches us in the Scriptures through the words of David: "One thing have I asked of the LORD, that will I seek after: that I may dwell in the house of the LORD all the days of my life, to gaze upon the beauty of the LORD and to inquire in his temple" (Ps. 27:4). As we see God's beauty and glory time and again, we will love him more.

Savor God's Love Again and Again

God's great love is part of his glory, of course, but it's worth pointing out specifically because of the explicit connection the Bible makes in this regard: "We love because he first loved us" (1 John 4:19). In the same way that our affection for our parents or grandparents swells as we recall all they have done for us and all the love they have shown us, our love for God is especially kindled as we think specifically of his love for us in Christ. God's love is so great that he didn't withhold his own Son but gave him up for us all so that we who were rebels, we who were his enemies, could have eternal life and joy rather than eternal death and misery. To truly taste that in our souls never gets old, and it kindles love for God again and again. Just as we strive to savor God's beauty, we should find ways to dwell on God's love for us.

Recall the Extent of God's Forgiveness Again and Again

There's a story from the Gospels that points specifically to how the recognition of what we've been forgiven of is tied to the love we feel for God:

One of the Pharisees asked [Jesus] to eat with him, and he went into the Pharisee's house and reclined at table. And behold, a woman of the city, who was a sinner, when she learned that he was reclining at table in the Pharisee's house, brought an alabaster flask of ointment, and standing behind him at his feet, weeping, she began to wet his feet with her tears and wiped them with the hair of her head and kissed his feet and anointed them with the ointment. Now when the Pharisee who had invited him saw this, he said to himself, "If this man were a prophet, he would have known who and what sort of woman this is who is touching him, for she is a sinner." And Jesus answering said to him, "Simon, I have something to say to you." And he answered, "Say it, Teacher."

"A certain moneylender had two debtors. One owed five hundred denarii, and the other fifty. When they could not pay, he canceled the debt of both. Now which of them will love him more?" Simon answered, "The one, I suppose, for whom he canceled the larger debt." And he said to him, "You have judged rightly." Then turning toward the woman he said to Simon, "Do you see this woman? I entered your house; you gave me no water for my feet, but she has wet my feet with her tears and wiped them with her hair. You gave me no kiss, but from the time I came in she has not ceased to kiss my feet. You did not anoint my head with oil, but she has anointed my feet with ointment. Therefore I tell you, her sins, which are many, are forgiven—for she loved much. But he who is forgiven little loves little." (Luke 7:36–47)

"She has been forgiven much because she loves much." Jesus isn't saying here that the woman's love has earned her forgiveness. Instead, he's saying that her love is the evidence that she's been forgiven, and her *great* love shows she's aware of just how much she's been forgiven.

How about you? What sins did God forgive when you became a Christian? How much has God forgiven you *since* you became a Christian? Maybe you would say, "I grew up in a Christian home, became a Christian at a young age, and have walked with Christ since. I wish I could feel the love that a converted drug addict feels for how much they've been forgiven." Nonsense. You are just not familiar enough with your heart. How many times has God seen you selfishly grasp for what you wanted at someone else's expense? How many times have you greedily coveted something or someone before being brought back to your senses? Friend, even if your life is squeaky-clean-looking from the outside, the list of the sins of your heart is as high as a mountain. But if you belong to Christ, God has forgiven *all* of them. Think about that and be humbled. Weep. But then let your heart be filled with love for the God who has freely forgiven you of so much. And then make this a practice you engage in nightly.

Recognize God as the Giver of Good and Pleasurable Gifts Again and Again

There are many pleasures we enjoy in life and many beautiful things we see and experience. It helps us grow in our love for God to consciously see God as the source of all these things as we experience them.

C. S. Lewis once wrote an essay about standing in a dark toolshed and looking at a beam of sunlight coming through a crack at the top of the door. He noted how it was a different experience to look *at* the beam than it was to go to the beam and look *along* it through the door and up to the sun above. While he was making a different point, this gets at what I'm talking about. In all our pleasures, in all the beautiful things we see, we don't want our delight to end with merely focusing on what it is we are enjoying. Instead, we want to "look along the beam"—to express our gratitude to God and to consider what this enjoyment says about him.

God loves to joyfully do good to others. It brings him delight. That's why your day is filled with thousands of pleasures, from the taste of your coffee to the feeling of the warm water on your skin in the shower to the enjoyment you get from the music you listen to on the way into work to the comfort you have in the love and care you experience from family members to the beauty of the flowers you see as you're driving through the neighborhood—and on and on and on. Do you know why our lives are filled with all those pleasures? It's because God loves to give. As we grow increasingly conscious of this as we experience those pleasures in a thousand different ways, we will grow in our love for God.

Even outside of the physical pleasures we enjoy and the beauty of creation, we ought to grow in enjoying God in this way in the music, books, and movies we enjoy. The real richness of the stories we enjoy comes from the fact that they serve as a sliver of a mirror that reflects the glory and beauty of God's character and ways, or the poignancy of the human condition in light of the hope that God offers.

Give Thanks to God for All His Gifts Again and Again

While this exhortation is closely related to the last, there is a distinction between the two. Recognizing God as the giver of our pleasures as we experience them is a "looking around" activity—we're relishing God in the moment of our pleasure. But here I'm thinking of thanking God for all his gifts as a "looking back" activity—relishing God as we reflect on all the pleasures he has gladly given us. Whenever we think back on the good the Lord has done for us, our love for him is stirred up again and reinforced. This practice of looking back and giving thanks is especially important because we tend to forget all the "small" pleasures and sights of beauty we experience every day.

Giving thanks is a biblical command, but the ultimate reason we are commanded to give thanks is not just because it's the right thing to do (though it is) or because it makes us aware of and grateful for the many good things we have received (though it does). The ultimate point of the Bible's command to give thanks is that we should see that God is a God who genuinely loves to give and who gladly and freely lavishes good gifts on us all. Every good gift or good pleasure that any human being experiences is happily given by him.

Along with acknowledging your sins and recognizing the forgiveness God extends to you, make it a nightly practice to thank God for the pleasures of food, for the joy and love of family and friends, and for all good things, tangible and intangible, you've received that day, and let it lead you to wonder and love for the God who has gladly given all of it to you.[3]

Slowly and Stealthily through Our Habits

Third, our love for God grows quietly in our habits. Of course, I've already alluded to habits as we've talked about how we should strive to enjoy God by practicing these things again and *again*. But here in this section, I'm talking especially about those habits where we don't always feel particular pleasure.[4] There are some habits where it seems like the pleasure we feel is small, and at times, the habit might even be unpleasant to us in some way. Yet each of these are means by which love for God grows quietly in our hearts. There are four particular habits of the Christian life where we need this encouragement: reading the Bible regularly, persevering in prayer, fellowshipping with other Christians, and participating in worship services.

---

3   Psalm 103 provides an excellent model for doing this.

4   Though, to be realistic, even as we strive to do some of the things we've talked about already—reflecting on the love of God, for instance—we don't consistently feel the same amount of pleasure each time we do them. Sadly, sometimes we feel no discernible pleasure at all. Such is life in this fallen world while sin still remains in our hearts.

Read the Bible Regularly

While reading the Bible is one of the foremost ways we can rejoice in who God is, there are also seasons of our lives where this seems incredibly dry to us. We all have valleys in our spiritual lives where we think, "I'm God's child. This is God's Word about his glory and goodness. Why do I feel so little pleasure in it, so little love for him?" When we do, the temptation will be to leave off reading his Word and to look elsewhere to try to replace the pleasure we once felt. Don't give in to this temptation.

I never knew that one of the greatest challenges of parenting is simply to get your child to eat their food at mealtime. As an adult, when good food is set in front of you, you eat! The problem is that you want to eat too much. But not kids. You might put the food that they loved last week in front of them for breakfast today, and it gets treated like cardboard. Total indifference. Part of this is simply being a child and being distracted by a thousand things that seem more interesting and pressing than eating. But part of it is that kids have no concept of the idea that you need to eat substantive food at mealtime so you don't get hungry or feel poorly later.

Just like eating meals when you don't feel terribly hungry is necessary to feel well and stay healthy, continuing to read the Bible when you feel emotionally dry is critical to keeping your love for God growing. In the same way that digestion happens and nutrients go to different parts of your body in a way you may be completely unaware of, when we "feed" on God's Word, the Spirit is growing our love for God in ways imperceptible to us.

The greatest discernible growth in my own spiritual life started the summer after my first year of seminary, when I started using Robert Murray M'Cheyne's Bible reading plan to read the Bible daily. Over the course of a year, M'Cheyne's reading plan takes you through the Old Testament once and the Psalms and the New Testament twice. Over the next handful of years, day in and day out, whether I felt like it or not, I read the Bible. Some days I was profoundly moved by God's glory. Other days I wasn't. But at the end of all those days of regularly reading the Bible, like a person who's eaten a steady diet of good food, my love for God was as strong and healthy as it's ever been.

Persevere in Prayer

Prayer often feels dry to us. Sometimes it seems as if no one is listening. Even more often, though we know God is listening, our minds are so distracted we feel like we're talking to ourselves more than we are to him. We don't know what to pray for. We're tempted to throw our hands up and fall back on passive satisfaction with the fact that God is sovereign and works everything out according to his good plans. While this is true, this reality is not meant to discourage our prayers to God.

Chapter Eight ▪ 99

Far from it, since God commands us to "pray without ceasing" (1 Thess. 5:17)!

All Christians can attest to struggling in prayer sometimes. But why should we press on in the habit? There are other reasons, of course, but let's focus on how prayer affects our love for God. How does prayer cause our love for God to grow? There are several ways.

First, there's adoration, or praising God in prayer. Adoration is not merely giving God his due but both the overflow of love and fuel for further love to grow. Think about the last time you went to a great restaurant. As you enjoyed the food, what did you say to those who were with you? Probably something along the lines of "Mmm! This food is *so* good!" over and over. Then, when you went to work the next day, how long was it before you had to tell someone about the restaurant? Not very long, if I had to guess from my own experience. Why is this? It wasn't out of any sense of duty. Rather, talking about what you experienced increased your pleasure in some way. You wouldn't have enjoyed what you experienced as much—you wouldn't have *loved* it as much—if you hadn't been able to praise it. This same dynamic takes place in our hearts when we praise God in prayer. In mysterious ways we don't fully grasp, we're actually increasing our pleasure in God and bringing it to completion by speaking of it.

Second, the freedom of childlike prayer warms our affections for God in the same way that a child pouring out his heart to a parent draws his heart close to them in love. Amazingly, we have this access to God as his children because he has adopted us in Christ. Perhaps you're thinking to yourself, "Yeah, that's not the reality of my prayer life. I wish I could pray that way." If you're a Christian, you can! Start your prayers the way that the Protestant Reformer Martin Luther encouraged, and let the truth of this reality sink into your heart:

> Although… you could rightly and properly be a severe judge over us sinners… now through your mercy implant in our hearts a comforting trust in your fatherly love, and let us experience the sweet and pleasant savor of a childlike certainty that we may joyfully call you Father, knowing and loving you and calling on you in every trouble.[5]

If you are a Christian, God is your Father, and you can pray this way. It doesn't matter if you're the newest or weakest Christian in the world. Don't believe otherwise—it is true. And the more you can pour your heart out in childlike prayer, the warmer your affections for God will be.

---

5   Martin Luther, "Personal Prayer Book," in *Luther's Works: Devotional Writings II*, ed. Gustav K. Wiencke (Minneapolis: Fortress Press, 1968), 43:29.

And third, of course, when we pray we can ask God to help us love him more. The bottom line is this, brothers and sisters: to grow in your love for God, don't give up. Keep praying!

Enjoy Fellowship with Other Christians

"Fellowship" is an abstract term we use a lot but aren't really sure what it means. Growing up in a small church, I always associated it with a potluck meal. That's not exactly right, of course, though it's not a stretch to say that eating together is a natural part of fellowship. The word "fellowship" is connected with the Greek word "*koinonia*" used in the New Testament. The root of that word, "*koine*," means "common." Fellowship, then, is the enjoying of all the good things that are ours together (or in common) in Christ.

This is one of the glories of Christianity we often don't see clearly in our culture of individualism. Too often we think about coming to worship services, Bible studies, or church events, and our focus is almost strictly on our own spiritual lives. "How is this going to strengthen and encourage *me* spiritually?" But Christianity is not a solo spiritual project. Christianity is not just about God being my Father but God being *our* Father. When we come together as Christians, we come together as a group of people—a family!—to whom God has given, in Christ, the spiritual blessings of forgiveness of our sins, reconciliation with God, access to

God in prayer, the inheritance of the kingdom of God, adoption by God as children, and the blessing of other brothers and sisters who encourage us, love us, and keep us from straying from him. When we come together, we are to experience and enjoy these blessings. That's fellowship.

But there's a first step that has to take place to fellowship with other Christians. We must spend time together. Before you can enjoy the benefits of being together, you must first *be together*. Particularly for those of us who are introverts, this isn't a habit we're naturally drawn to. Even if we've experienced great joy being with other Christians, we can still find ourselves averse to the thought of going to another gathering. But this is a habit we need to nurture. While there are several reasons why, let's just consider it from the standpoint of growing in our love for God. Being around other Christians is a significant source of fuel for the fire of our love for God. Why? Because seeing God at work in *their* lives will further *our* love for God.

When you hear how Christ is ministering to your brother or sister in their trial or grief, you will love him more. When you see the joy and hope that Christ continues to give them, you will love him more. When you hear what Christ is teaching them and how he is enabling them to overcome their harmful desires, you will love him more. When you hear how Christ is bringing peace to their families and relationships, you will love him more. And when you see how Christ is at work ministering to his people as they love one another, you will love him more. In short, spending time with other Christians enables you to see the Lord at his glorious and good work in a thousand ways you wouldn't see otherwise.

Participate in Worship Services

A sad reality in the American church today is witnessing the two opposing ways in which so many Christians seem to approach their church's weekly worship service. Some Christians see the worship service as a strict duty: "I have to go to church on Sunday." This approach sees the service as just another religious obligation that must be done. They see little joy in it. Others see it as an optional choice among many others: "Maybe I'll go to church on Sunday if I'm up on time and I don't have other things going on." They see little value in it. Brothers and sisters, this shouldn't be!

Week to week, there is no event in the life of the Christian that is as important as the worship service, nothing which as the potential to impact one's love for God more. Think about it. Every week, the worship service gives you the opportunity to experience almost all the pleasures we've discussed—savoring God's glory, relishing his love, being reminded of his forgiveness, recognizing him as the giver of all good gifts, and thanking him. And then there is prayer and fellowship as well. If you want your love for God to stay warm and grow, then don't skip worship service!

Don't Throw Water on the Fire of Your Love for God

Finally, if you want to keep your love for God hot and see it grow, you must not douse it by toying with sin. Engaging in and delighting in what is evil will inevitably dampen the fire of your affection love for God. There is always some pleasure in sin, or else it wouldn't be appealing to us. But you cannot relish what is good while you are relishing what is evil. It's simply not possible.

Sin darkens our apprehension of God's love and dampens our love for him. Like a child who doesn't find it pleasant to come to a parent she knows is going to discipline her, we experience the same when we willfully sin.

If you want your love for God to stay warm and to grow, you must fight temptation and sin. You must put to death the desires of your sinful nature, or they will put to death your love for God.

Helping Others Grow in Their Love for God

So, we've talked about the dynamics of how affection love grows and remains warm. We've talked about the "what" and the "how" of the practices and habits we need to engage in to help our love for God grow. But what about helping others grow in their love for God? How do we make disciples who love God more and more?

Here are several ways (though, again, not all the ways) that every Christian can help other Christians love God more.

Love God Deeply and Spend Time with Others

Have you ever heard someone talk about a topic they love? Even if you had little interest in it yourself, you can't help but find yourself fascinated, can you? When someone has enthusiasm for what they're speaking about, it has a magnetic effect. Overhear a conversation like that in a crowded room, and you want to be a part of it. This enthusiasm is part of the appeal of great teachers—in fact, it's hard to imagine any great teacher who isn't extremely enthusiastic about their subject. It's similarly contagious to be around someone who loves God sincerely and enthusiastically.

Part of this, of course, is because a person who truly loves God reflects who God is, and that beauty draws us toward them. We want to be like them because we see that beauty. But being around them also makes us think to ourselves, "If they love God this much, he must be really glorious!"

Talk Often about God's Goodness and Beauty

An advertisement for a runaway slave ran in the *Camden Journal* of Camden, South Carolina, on March 4, 1837. Mr. J. Bishop placed the following: "Ranaway a negro named Arthur, has a considerable scar across his breast and each arm, made by a knife; loves to talk much of the goodness of God."[6]

I'm moved every time I read that short description of this runaway slave. Even though he was experiencing the brutal, soul-crushing realities of chattel slavery, one of the primary means of identifying him was that he "loves to talk much of the goodness of God." What a man! What a faith! Think about how many people must have been struck by the thought upon meeting him, "How astonishing must this God be who is able to fill a man with joy at his goodness in the midst of slavery!" All of us as Christians should strive to be like this brother named Arthur—not to display our righteousness but to encourage others to love God too.

Try to find ways in your conversations with other Christians to acknowledge the goodness of God, whether it's by speaking of his goodness in general or of some way he has specifically been good to you. Remember, it is experiencing pleasure—in this case, the pleasure of experiencing God's goodness and beauty—that draws forth our love. Think of ways you can point to Christ's glory in your conversations. Tell others how you've seen God's glory and goodness lately—in your study of Scripture, your personal life,

---

6   "Runaway Slave Newspaper Advertisements," Genealogy Trails, accessed October 16, 2020, http://www.genealogytrails.com/main/slaveadverts.html.

or in the world around you (nature, books, movies). Encouraging one another to consider what is excellent and praiseworthy (Philippians 4) and reminding each other of where that excellence finds its starting point is a great way to encourage one another in the love of God.

Remind Others That God Loves Them

Toward the end of my time in seminary, I went through a pretty brutal time of spiritual anxiety and depression. Convictions I had seemed so sure of were suddenly uncertain, and I found myself groping in the dark as to who God was and where I stood with him—not exactly fertile grounds for a thriving love for God.

In my church's congregation was a dear old couple in their eighties who were very warm, mature Christians. I don't remember many sermons from my time in that church, but I do remember one very short, profound sermon that this older lady, Dot, preached to me. She asked me how I was doing, and I stammered out some sort of response indicating my struggles. All she said in reply was simply, "Kevin, God loves you very much. Don't forget that." It was as if heaven itself had spoken. I went for days on the strength of what those two sentences did in my soul.

Dietrich Bonhoeffer, the German theologian who died at the hands of the Nazis, stated this truth profoundly:

God has put his Word into the mouth of men in order that it may be communicated to other men. When one person is struck by the Word, he speaks it to others. God has willed that we should seek and find His living Word in the witness of a brother, in the mouth of a man. Therefore, the Christian needs another Christian who speaks God's Word to him. He needs him again and again when he becomes uncertain and discouraged, for by himself he cannot help himself without belying the truth. He needs his brother as a bearer and proclaimer of the divine word of salvation. He needs his brother solely because of Jesus Christ. The Christ in his own heart is weaker than the Christ in the word of his brother; his own heart is uncertain, his brother's is sure.[7]

A simple word from someone on the "outside" goes a long way in helping our hearts feel and respond rightly. So, remind others of God's love in order to help them to love him—it may do far more good than you ever could imagine.[8]

---

7 Dietrich Bonhoeffer, *Life Together*, trans. John W. Doberstein (New York: Harper & Brothers, 1954), 22–23.

8 I've heard another brother and friend of mine console several struggling, grieving Christians with the sincere and simple affirmation "God is for you." It was profoundly effective.

A Final Word to Pastors and Worship Leaders

What I've shared above are ways that every Christian can help make disciples by encouraging their brothers and sisters in Christ to grow in love for God. But here, I want to speak to pastors and worship leaders specifically about the weekly worship service and the preaching that's part of it. As I've already mentioned, probably no greater opportunity exists to form Christians in their love for God than the weekly worship service. For those of us who are church leaders, then, God has given us the high privilege and the sobering responsibility to prepare and conduct those services in such a way that this takes place. What can we do to ensure that the members of our churches are being formed to love God as they come to worship week after week?

It should go without saying that the first thing we need to do is pray. Pray for God to give us wisdom as we lead the church each week. Pray for the Spirit of God to work as the church gathers for worship, stirring up love for God and for what is good in the hearts of the people.

Second, we should recognize the formative power of a weekly retelling and reliving of the gospel in the hearts of our church members. In the same way that we find personal habits forming and deepening our loves, what we do weekly in our worship services (our "habits") has the power to do the same. Therefore, rather than allowing our services to be haphazardly structured, we ought to organize our services around a retelling of the gospel each week. After all, as we've said numerous times now—we love in response to God's love. Therefore, hearing the story of God's love in Christ each week—albeit told through the lens of different Scripture readings, songs, and sermons—causes us to respond in love. We need to plan our worship services with a gospel rhythm to them and arrange opportunities for the congregation to experience the various pleasures that have already been discussed.[9]

I know there will be leaders in liturgical churches (churches with a more overt structure to their services) who will read those last couple of paragraphs and say, "Brother, you are late to the game! We've been doing this for ages." As a Baptist, I can only acknowledge this is true and tip my hat. But there is one thing I would add from my limited experience in liturgical churches. While it is true that these churches have services structured around the gospel, even then, the congregants often aren't aware of it. Church leaders must make sure their church members understand what's happening and why that structure is in place. Understanding that we're reliving the gospel story each week (call, confession of sin, assurance of pardon, hearing God's Word, responding in faith, and being sent out—or, alternately,

---

9 For a good resource on this, see Mike Cosper, *Rhythms of Grace: How the Church's Worship Tells the Story of the Gospel* (Wheaton, IL: Crossway, 2013).

creation, fall, redemption, and consummation) helps us to grasp it more clearly and savor it more deeply.

Third—and this is to pastors in particular—we must preach to stir up love for God. This needs to be one of the primary aims of our preaching. We're not just informing congregants' minds (though that's important), nor are we simply encouraging them to practically apply God's Word to their lives (though that's important too). But just as essential is preaching that holds up God's glory and beauty for the church to see. This is why Paul preached "the unsearchable riches of Christ," so that those who heard would relish the Christ he proclaimed. Our preaching must do the same![10]

---

10   If I could offer a simple model of preaching, it would be E-G-A: (1) *Explain* God's Word so the hearers understand it; (2) *Glorify* God's Word so the hearers are awakened to its beauty and profundity (and that of God himself as he's revealed through it) and so are stirred to love God and the truth; and (3) *Apply* God's Word so the hearers respond in faith and trust.

Chapter Nine

How Do We Grow in Trust in God?

So we've gained a better understanding of what it means to love God, how that love grows, and what we ought to do to help that love grow. Now we move on to trusting God. As I discussed in chapter 5, it is true in one regard that we either trust God or we don't, in the sense of decisively trusting in Jesus Christ to deliver us from our sins and our sinfulness as well as trusting in his wisdom so we commit ourselves to doing what he says. Every person has either decisively trusted in Jesus in this way or they haven't. But it's also true for Christian disciples that even after this decisive moment of trusting in Jesus, we face a lifetime of struggle with doubts, fears, pride, and sinful desires that keep us from trusting in him and growing in that trust. This chapter is about how we go about fighting that fight. And just as we started our chapter on how to grow in love for God with a discussion about the general dynamics of love—how we grow in our love for anyone or anything—it's also helpful to start in a similar way when it comes to trust. Generally speaking, how do we grow in trusting others?

I had a good friend in college who I never thought would be a friend. With most good friends, there's an instant rapport. We realize fairly quickly that we're drawn to that person and have things in common. This friend was different, though. We hadn't interacted much, but the times we had left me with a distinct impression of him—he seemed shifty. I didn't like his looks. Since I've never told him this, I'll refrain from naming names to protect the innocent. But when we were thrown into a group together and I got to know him better, I soon saw that my initial perceptions of him were dead wrong. Over time, he became a trusted friend.

Think about a good friend of yours, someone you trust deeply. You might have had an initial, minimal kind of trust in them that grew as you got to know them more. You learned more about them and their history. You learned that they were dependable in the past. And over the course of time, you learned their character. Over and over, their actions proved they were sincere, honest, and trustworthy and that they were wise enough for you to bank on their counsel to you. Maybe this trust grew in small ways at first, but the more you trusted them, the more you were willing to trust them with, and your trust grew even greater when you found them trustworthy in

114 ■ *A Simple Model of Discipleship*

those bigger things. Growing in our trust in God is very similar to this. We grow in our trust in God as we increasingly come to know him. We grow in our trust of God by growing in our knowledge of his character, wisdom, and faithfulness. This knowledge comes through understanding his Word and through personal experience, both our own and that of others.

So how do we grow in our trust in God? Here are four important ways.

Learn of God's Character, Wisdom, and Faithfulness from the Bible

Just as if we were meeting someone new, we have to come to know that God can be trusted. As we've alluded, the place where this trust starts is seeing God's desire for our good in sending his Son (John 3:16). Then, recognizing God loves us so much that he didn't spare his own Son for us, we come to believe that he will do whatever it takes to do us good (Rom. 8:32). But the human heart is so buffeted by doubts and suspicions about God's character that it needs more than grasping this truth at just one particular point in life. We need to steadily grow in our knowledge of God's character and faithfulness and frequently be reminded of it.

As we read through the Bible, we learn that God deals honestly and mercifully with all who come to him sincerely, even when we come to him after we have sinned grievously. One of the most astonishing demonstrations of this is in the life of Ahab when he was king of Israel. Ahab just looked the other way while his wife, Jezebel, conspired to have an innocent man killed merely so Ahab could have his vineyard. The word of the Lord comes to the prophet Elisha, who goes and pronounces to Ahab the judgment that God is going to bring upon him. Then the biblical writer of 1 Kings adds this side comment:

> There was none who sold himself to do what was evil in the sight of the LORD like Ahab, whom Jezebel his wife incited. He acted very abominably in going after idols, as the Amorites had done, whom the LORD cast out before the people of Israel. (21:25–26)

All this is to set up what happened next: Ahab actually repented! He responded to God, putting on sackcloth, fasting, and humbling himself. This is shocking, but not nearly as astounding as what happened next.

> And the word of the LORD came to Elijah the Tishbite, saying, "Have you seen how Ahab has humbled himself before me? Because he has humbled himself before me, I will not bring disaster in his days; but in his son's days I will bring the disaster upon his house." (vv. 28–29)

Wow. We expect a conclusion like one in an action movie where the archvillain finally gets what's coming to him, but when Ahab sincerely responded to the Lord, the Lord met him in mercy. Throughout the Bible, we learn that if we come to God in sincerity, we can fully trust him to respond in mercy and for our good.

We also need to see that God has a long and proven track record of keeping his promises for the good of his people. We'll learn this if we're willing to read and study the Bible. When the people of Israel settled in the land that God had promised to their forefathers, after being enslaved in Egypt for four hundred years and delivered by the power of God, it's the utter trust-worthiness of God that the biblical writer ensures we don't miss:

> Thus the LORD gave to Israel all the land that he swore to give to their fathers. And they took possession of it, and they settled there. And the LORD gave them rest on every side just as he had sworn to their fathers. Not one of all their enemies had withstood them, for the LORD had given all their enemies into their hands. *Not one word of all the good promises that the LORD had made to the house of Israel had failed: all came to pass.* (Josh. 21:43–45, italics added)

Go to Worship Service Each Week

I've already extolled the virtues of attending worship weekly. Here, let's ask specifically: How does going to your local church's worship service each week foster trust in God?

First, the very presence of other Christians helps our trust in God. We find that our trust is strengthened when we are around other people who trust God and to whom God is demonstrating himself as trustworthy.

Second, as you sing songs that declare the faithfulness, wisdom, and proven character of God and as you hear the Scriptures read and preached, you will be reminded of all the reasons you have to trust God. A worship service is a place where trust in God is naturally (and supernaturally) encouraged, often without us even being aware of it.

Spend Time with Other Christians

One of the sad aspects of so many of our relationships in the church is their superficiality. We see each other once a week, maybe twice, and often don't go beyond exchanging pleasantries. We'll never experience the encouragement that God intends Christians to give to one another unless we move past that superficiality. The only way to do so is to spend time together—enough time that we know what's happening in one another's lives and hearts and establish the trust to share that with one another.

118 ▪ *A Simple Model of Discipleship*

When we do, we'll find there is great encouragement for us to trust God more as we see him at work faithfully and wisely in the lives of his children. So make the time and the effort to be with other brothers and sisters in Christ, and be open to the Spirit's work in opening up your hearts to one another.

It will also encourage you to spend time with Christians who have already died. I'm talking about reading their biographies, of course. It is inspiring, yes, to read of the faith of Christians throughout history and the great acts of love for others that faith led them to. But reading their stories is often a profound testimony to the faithfulness of God. Consider John G. Paton as an example.

Paton was a nineteenth-century missionary to the New Hebrides (a group of islands in the South Pacific now known as Vanuatu) at a point in time when cannibals inhabited the islands. Before he had been there a year, Paton's wife died shortly after giving birth to their first son. Seventeen days later, the child died. Paton was utterly grief-stricken, but Jesus met him there in his promise never to leave him nor forsake him. Paton wrote, "But for Jesus, and the fellowship He vouchsafed me there, I must have gone mad and died beside that lonely grave!"[1] Even there on that desolate island, so far from

---

1   John Paton, *John G. Paton: Missionary to the New Hebrides, An Autobiography* Edited by His Brother, ed. James Paton (Edinburgh: Banner of Truth, 1965, orig. 1889, 1891), 80.

Chapter Nine ▪ 119

any sympathetic and like-minded others, Paton found that Jesus was faithful to his promise. And it wasn't the only time.

Paton's life was almost constantly under threat of death from one group of hostile natives or another. Once a man rushed at him with an axe and would have killed him were it not for another native Paton had been working with, who grabbed a spade and warded off the attacker. Another night there was a mob of villagers hunting him. Not knowing who he could trust, Paton climbed up into a tree and later shared his remarkable experience:

> I climbed into the tree and was left there alone in the bush. The hours I spent there live all before me as if it were but yesterday. I heard the frequent discharging of muskets, and the yells of Savages. Yet I sat there among the branches, as safe as in the arms of Jesus. Never, in all my sorrows, did my Lord draw nearer to me, and speak more soothingly in my soul, than when the moonlight flickered among those chestnut leaves, and the night air played on my throbbing brow, as I told all my heart to Jesus. Alone, yet not alone! If it be to glorify my God, I will not grudge to spend many nights alone in such a tree, to feel again my Savior's spiritual presence, to enjoy His consoling fellowship. If thus thrown back upon your own soul, alone, all

alone, in the midnight, in the bush, in the very embrace of death itself, have you a Friend that will not fail you then?[2]

You do have such a friend. If you are a Christian, the same Christ who was with Paton in that tree has promised to walk with you throughout every moment of your life. You can bank on the fact that this is true. And there are plenty of Christian biographies that will help remind you of it.

Live on a Steady Diet of God's Promises
We've talked thus far about three general ways to grow in our trust of God: learn (and be reminded of) the Bible for the sake of growing in your knowledge of his character, wisdom, and faithfulness; regularly attend worship services; and spend time with other Christians. This fourth way is much more specific—learn and bank on God's specific promises in the Bible.

I must confess that most of the books I've picked up that had a title along the lines of *The Promises of God* have sorely disappointed me. These books are presumably filled with all the promises of God from the Scriptures. The problem is, they usually aren't. They are filled with a number of verses or passages of Scripture, but many of them aren't promises at all. They're statements

---

2   Paton, 200.

of a particular truth, akin to "The LORD is gracious and merciful, slow to anger and abounding in steadfast love" (Ps. 145:8). This is a beautiful truth, and one worth dwelling on, but it's not a *promise* from God. Yet there are plenty of promises in the Bible, and those promises play an important part in our growth in Christlikeness.

> His divine power has granted to us all things that pertain to life and godliness, through the knowledge of him who called us to his own glory and excellence, by which he has granted to us his precious and very great promises, so that through them you may become partakers of the divine nature, having escaped from the corruption that is in the world because of sinful desire. (2 Peter 1:3–4)

It's through God's "precious and very great promises" that we may become partakers of the divine nature (that our characters may become like God's), and said promises help us escape from the corruption in the world because of sinful desire. The way this works is that there is pleasure that comes from believing in God's promises and a certainty that we will possess this good thing he promises. Even though we don't fully possess it yet, this certainty is like possessing that good in some small way. There is joy in anticipating what will be ours (the same way we find delight in anticipating our beach vacation in

122 ▪ *A Simple Model of Discipleship*

two months). This pleasure helps us turn away from the deceitful pleasure that sin offers us here and now. So being reminded of God's promises in our temptation is a means of pitting pleasure against pleasure —the pleasure that God offers versus the pleasure that sin offers. Embracing the pleasure of God's promise means turning away from the pleasure of sin. The more and more we do this, of course, the more our character is formed to be like Christ's.

Again, God's promises are not merely statements of truth in the Bible (as wonderful and important as those are). They are, as one renowned preacher said, the great "shalls" and "wills" of Scripture. There are *hundreds* of these promises scattered throughout the Scriptures like diamonds. For example:

> Fear not, for I am with you;
> be not dismayed, for I am your God;
> I *will* strengthen you, I *will* help you,
> I *will* uphold you with my righteous right hand.
> (Isa. 41:10, emphasis added)

> Call upon me in the day of trouble;
> I *will* deliver you, and you *shall* glorify me.
> (Ps. 50:15, emphasis added)

How do you grow in trust? You need to know these promises! The more you rest in these promises and the more you see them come to pass in your life, the more you will trust God to fulfill every promise he has made, even in the midst of the most adverse circumstances you will face.

How to Help Others Grow in Their Trust in God

In order to make disciples, we talked in the last chapter about how we can help others grow in their love for God. Now we turn our attention to making disciples by helping others grow in trust. In what ways we can help others grow in their trust in God?

Share Stories of God's Faithfulness in Your Life, Whether "Big" or "Small"

If you want to help others in your church grow in their trust in God, talk about what he has done and is doing in your life. Yes, God intends that you, ordinary Christian that you are, should be a great encouragement to your brother's or sister's faith.

We're often hesitant to share about what's happening in our lives because it seems so mundane at times. If we had a story like John G. Paton in the tree with murderers all around in the dark, then sure, we could share *that*, but our routine week of working and getting the kids to school and soccer practice? I want to encourage you that even hearing "small" answers to prayer or the ways you've seen God be faithful in your ordinary life are a great encouragement to your brothers and sisters in Christ. It bolsters our trust to hear of his faithfulness to you.

Personally speaking, this is probably the most encouraging aspect of the weekly church small group my family is part of. Week after week, my trust in God is strengthened by hearing how he's faithfully at work in the lives of the other members of our group. So, speak up and share—your fellow disciples need to hear how God is at work in your life!

Remind Others of God's Promises

As you remember others in your church, think of the specific promises of God that would encourage them in their circumstances. As you invest the time to learn and memorize God's promises, be spurred on by the knowledge that you're not just learning them for yourself. They will be a remarkable means for loving your brothers and sisters in Christ when you hold out these promises to them in their struggles and darkness.

Some of the most deeply meaningful experiences of my Christian life have been just this—the joy of holding out a promise from our never-failing God for a fellow Christian to find hope and rest in in the midst of great struggle. One such instance occurred with my dear and valiant brother Chad Southward.

Chad was one of the most remarkable men I've ever known. He was born with cystic fibrosis and spent a lot of his childhood in and out of the hospital. When I met Chad, he and his wife, Lauren, had recently moved in right across the street from us. At that point, he had already had two double-lung transplants. The remarkable thing about Chad, though, was that apart from some of the physical indicators, you would never know it. He never let his illness define him or cast a shadow over his life. He lived with zest (he loved colorful clothes) and loved to laugh and to make you laugh. Early in my pastorate, I baptized Chad and Lauren as they expressed their decisive trust in Christ and their commitment to follow him.

A handful of years later, Chad's body began to reject his second set of lungs. Because he had done so well with the previous two transplants, Duke University was willing to make him a candidate for a third double-lung transplant, the first one they had ever done. On Thanksgiving Day of 2016, the call came that a donor was available. The third transplant was performed—and was a success! Chad fought like a tiger to make it through therapy and was home in time for the birth of his second son in March. Not long after, he was back at work.

Later in the year, though, there were indicators that things were not going well with the third set of lungs. Eventually, his body rejected them, and the doctors were left with no options. But Chad faced this as he had lived his life: with courage, hope, and faith. This is not to say that he didn't need help. His wife and family and our church family were there with him through it all. I particularly had the opportunity to have earnest conversations with Chad about life and death and to have the joy of holding out Jesus's promise to him again and again: "I will never leave you nor forsake you" (Heb. 13:5). I saw Chad embrace that promise, and when he died in May of 2018, he died in faith that even then his Savior would be true to his word.

He was right.

Pastors, Preach for Trust!

Finally, I want to share a word with pastors. The messages you preach each week are a profound opportunity to help those in your church grow in trusting God more deeply. This means being attentive to and highlighting for your congregation the different ways the Bible points to the trustworthiness of God. They (and we) need to hear again and again, *"You can trust God."*

Preaching for trust also means ensuring that all our appeals for obedience and application are grounded in trust in God. In Romans 1, Paul wrote that through Christ he and the other apostles had "received grace and apostleship to bring about the *obedience of faith* for the sake of his name among all the nations" (v. 5, emphasis added). This little phrase is critical because it makes clear that God intends obedience to him to flow out of faith and trust in him.

So when we preach, we should make it a point to never leave a command of God hanging out there alone—"this is God's law, so you need to do it" or "God says this, and you need to obey." While both of those statements are technically true, leaving them hanging alone could produce an obedience that is not pleasing to God. God does not want his children to obey him because he is stronger than they are and they're afraid they'll be "beat up" if they don't listen.

As we preach, we need to ground our calls for obedience to God in the reminder that God knows what is good and seeks your good; therefore, you should obey him—even when you don't feel like it—because you trust him.

At the same time, we need to ground our calls to obedience to God in the specific promises of God. How do those in the church who are struggling financially obey the command to not be anxious about anything? By hearing and believing what God promises his people through the apostle Paul in Philippians 4:19: "My God will supply every need of yours according to his riches in glory in Christ Jesus." How does the brother who has just been diagnosed with cancer keep from succumbing to fearfulness and despair? By remembering and believing (again and again!) that the Lord promises in Isaiah 41:10, "Fear not, for I am with you; be not dismayed, for I am your God; I will strengthen you, I will help you, I will uphold you with my righteous right hand."

May the Lord give us grace and wisdom as we proclaim his character and promises so his people's trust in him is ever more grounded and growing.

Chapter Ten

How Do We Grow in Fear of God?

We live in an age of irreverence. Think about it: Who is deeply respected in our society? There was a time in America not that long ago when we respected clergymen, teachers, policemen, and politicians. But the era of respect for authority has ended. An incident in my youth typifies this shattering of respect for me. One day in high school study hall, our teacher, an older gentleman, called down one of the boys in our class for being rowdy. The boy promptly jumped up and screamed an expletive at our teacher. My jaw hit the floor. I was shocked that someone my age would speak to an authority figure that way. I didn't realize then that our entire society was on a boat steadily drifting in that direction. Now the closest we come to reverence is how we feel about athletes and celebrities.

But we're ready to heap scorn on them, too, if they ever take a strong stance on a political position or moral issue that we disagree with. In short, there's no one we truly stand in awe of.

Of course, that's not necessarily wrong when it comes to other people. But when we lose a sense of awe altogether, we are in dangerous waters because there is One we ought to always stand in awe of. God is not a doting, sentimental old grandfather—he is a consuming fire of holiness and power, and to treat him lightly is foolish.

> For who in the skies can be compared to the LORD?
> Who among the heavenly beings is like the LORD,
> *a God greatly to be feared in the council of the holy ones,*
> *and awesome above all who are around him?*
> (Ps. 89:6–7, italics added)

In the same way that we started the chapters on how to grow in our love for and trust in God, I'd like to start here by talking about the dynamics of fear or reverence. How do we grow in deep respect for anyone or anything?

One way we grow in our respect for someone or something is by growing in our understanding of its power. Last year, our family completed a lengthy renovation project on our house. For three years, we did demolition, dug footings, installed subfloors, the whole nine yards. We did have contractors come and do some of the work and—okay, full confession—even the work that "we" did on the house was under the supervision of skilled and generous friends. I was largely a gopher, but a gopher who learned a lot. One of the things I learned was how to wire the inside of a house. I crawled under our addition, running wire from receptacle to receptacle and then wiring the outlets to those receptacles. (Amazingly, they still work!)

During the project, one of the things I gained was a healthy respect—reverence, even—for the power of electricity. I already possessed that to a certain degree as we began the project; I didn't have any desire to mess with the wiring on the main panel. I was intellectually aware of the power of the electricity running through that panel. But by the end of the project, I learned the power of electricity from experience when someone accidentally flipped a breaker on a 220-volt hot water heater wire that hadn't yet been fully rewired. It sounded like someone fired a shotgun, and all the lights went out in the house. Needless to say, after experiencing the power of electricity in that way, my respect for it deepened.

So, one way we grow in reverence is to recognize someone's or something's power. But we also grow in reverence as we recognize the holiness of someone's character. By holiness I mean the righteousness or the moral goodness of a person, particularly when that holiness carries with it the sense of an otherworldly goodness.

We saw this type of reverence in the way the public responded to Pope Francis when he visited America in 2015. Massive crowds gathered wherever the pope traveled, hoping to get a glimpse of the man deemed "His Holiness." One *New York Times* article recounted the story of a mother whose baby was blessed by the pope. The experience, and her response, is the epitome of reverence:

> As they waited, Ms. Chuquirima, came up with a plan: Should the pope drive by, she told her group, everyone should yell the pope's name in unison in the hope he might turn to them.
>
> At about 3:30 p.m. they heard the distant roar of the crowd, and that sound swept closer like an approaching storm, tracking the movement of the pope's convoy—a thunderous wave of adulation.
>
> It was headed toward their spot of grass. Ms. Chuquirima lifted Noah Gabriel, in his baptism clothes of a white singlet and white beanie, into her arms.
>
> The popemobile came into view, and the group saw a member of the pope's security detail carrying a baby to the pope for a blessing.

Ms. Chuquirima allowed herself a thought: Maybe they would also pick Noah Gabriel.

"But I didn't think he would stop," she recalled. She kept yelling and whistling all the same. "Papa! Papa!" she hollered, using the Spanish word for pope.

Francis was looking in the other direction as he drew abreast of the group but one of his security guards spotted Noah Gabriel and headed toward him.

"As he got close, my legs started shaking," Ms. Chuquirima recalled. "Even as I tell the story now, my legs are shaking."

The baby was lifted from her arms and, overwhelmed with emotion, she clutched the guardrail to prevent herself from collapsing. "I was yelling and crying, saying, 'God loves me. God loves me.' I feel like God touched me, he gave me his hand."

She was so overcome with emotion, she was unable to see what happened next: The security guard carried Noah Gabriel to the pope, who touched and kissed his head. The group from San Aloysius Church was ecstatic.

Moments later, the baby was back in his mother's arms.

"I felt like my son was an angel," Ms. Chuquirima said. Still overwhelmed by the memory an hour and a half after the event, she started crying once again. "It's a blessing for our family, for our parish. I feel like God chose this baby, to be a martyr, to be something special."[1]

When we are in the presence of someone we believe is profoundly good and always does the right thing, don't we feel a sense of reverence? We sense our own shortcomings and stand in awe of such righteousness. But remember, this type of fear is not a fear that causes us to shrink away from the object of our fear but to be drawn toward it. Even though we stand in awe of this type of righteousness to the point of trembling, we find our hearts drawn toward this person rather than away from them. We know that our lives cannot be complete without experiencing this righteousness and goodness.

---

1   Kirk Semple, "A Baby is Blessed, and a Mother Is Overcome," *New York Times*, September 27, 2015, accessed August 19, 2020, https://www.nytimes.com/live/pope-visit-2015/how-it-feels-to-have-your-baby-kissed-by-the-pope. I'm not arguing that this type of reverence for the pope is justified or healthy, only that it provides us with a clear example of what reverence looks like.

Growing in the Fear of God

How do we grow in the fear of God, then? The short answer is by recognizing and experiencing his holiness and power. But where and how does that happen? What should you do to put yourself in the way of these experiences?

Gather to Worship Weekly with Other Christians

I suspect you're picking up on a theme by this point. I've already made the case for the critical place of the worship service in growing in love for and trust in God. It's also essential for growing in the fear of God. Just as the worship service reminds us of God's beauty while stirring our love, and of his faithfulness while calling for our trust, it also reminds us of God's power and holiness and draws forth our reverence for him.

But can't this happen in other places and in different ways? Absolutely, and it does. I will point to a few of them shortly. But why would you pass up the place and time where God has designed and appointed for this to take place each week?

The fact is that if you are profoundly struck by God's holiness and power in any given week it will most likely occur during your church's worship service (assuming, of course, that you attend services and that the service is conducted in reverence for God). This is because, while God is sovereign and can make his presence known wherever and whenever he pleases, there can be no doubt—based on the

Scriptures and the experiences of God's people throughout the history of the church—that the usual place and time God makes his presence most profoundly known is when his people are gathered to worship him.

Nowhere is God so palpably present as where his people gather to worship him in truth and reverence. If you neglect this gathering, you are missing the most profound opportunity you have to keep the fear of God kindled and growing in your heart.

Read or Listen to God's Word Frequently

In Isaiah 66:1–2, the Lord tells his people that he is not looking for them to build a majestic house for him to impress him. Rather, he is looking for the humble believer who "trembles at [his] word." God looks to the one who fears when he or she hears God's Word. And there is much indeed in the Bible to strike our hearts with the awesomeness of God—both his power and his holiness.

In the Bible, we see God's power. In the Bible, we learn that God created the universe out of nothing. In the Bible, we learn that God brought his people out of slavery in Egypt. In the Bible, we learn that God displayed even greater power and delivered his people from slavery to sin. In the Bible, we learn that God has the power to raise the dead. When we see the power of God revealed in the Scriptures again and again, we will fear him.

In the Bible, we also see God's holiness. We learn that because of that holiness no man can see God's face

136 ▪ *A Simple Model of Discipleship*

and live. We hear the story of how Uzzah grabbed the ark of God and died as he misjudged the distance between his sinfulness and God's holiness (2 Sam. 6:6–7). In the Bible, we come to understand that not only is God so holy he cannot do what is evil, he is so holy he cannot even be *tempted* to do what is evil. There is no place whatsoever in his character where evil might find a footing to tempt God—none even exists. He is that holy, that *good*. When we first realize God's holiness—and, later, as we are reminded of it in the Scriptures—we stand in fear of the Lord.

Get Out into Nature and Marvel at God's Power in What You See

In Romans 1:20, the apostle Paul writes that God's "invisible attributes, namely, his eternal power and divine nature, have been clearly perceived, ever since the creation of the world, in the things that have been made." God's power has been made known (and is being made known) in all that he has created.

In 2000, a friend of mine got tickets to the U.S. Open golf tournament out at Pebble Beach in California. A Virginia native, I had never visited California before (nor had he), so we decided to fly into San Jose and drive down the Pacific Coast Highway to Pebble Beach. It felt like an oven when we arrived in San Jose, with the temps somewhere in the mid-nineties. But within an hour, we had made our way to the coast, where the temperature dropped to the low seventies and where I was introduced to a coastline unlike any I had ever experienced before. Growing up, my family had always vacationed in Myrtle Beach, South Carolina, where the beach is flat and the surf often laps at the shore. In the summer, unless there's a storm, it's almost always the picture of docile family fun. But if Myrtle Beach was a tame kitten, the Pacific coast was a tiger—and a rather miffed one at that. Massive rocks rose out of the ocean, and majestic cliffs dropped precipitously down to the water, with the surf pounding vigorously against them both. Stretches of beach dotted the shoreline, though nearly all of them were desolate. It was truly awe-inspiring, especially in light of what I had understood before as "the beach." I remember thinking of the sheer power of God to create it all—of how much bigger he was than I had previously experienced—and standing in awe of him.

Unfortunately, we now spend our nights almost exclusively under the light of our screens rather than the light of the moon and our days under an electronic glow rather than the glow of the sun. Growing in the fear of God doesn't require us to shun our electronic devices and entertainment altogether, but it surely means we'll have to fight their allure and their tendency to take over our lives in order to get out into the astonishing world God created.

Be Discerning in What You Read and Watch

The stories we encounter in books, television shows, and movies carry with them a profound power to affect our hearts and shape what we love, hate, and fear. We find ourselves empathizing, sympathizing, and really liking certain characters and wanting the story to turn out well for them. Yet sometimes what they really want (a certain longing that we ourselves can identify with) is ultimately one that God, in his wisdom and love, has forbidden. This is dangerous ground for us because the creator of this story may portray the fulfillment of this longing as a good thing, and we may find our hearts relishing that. Of course, this doesn't mean we will reject God's Word outright about a particular matter, but it can make his Word seem forbidding and restrictive and strengthen a love in our hearts for what we ought not love.

The movie *The Bridges of Madison County* is a perfect example of this. An Iowa farmwife in a loveless marriage meets a *National Geographic* photographer on assignment to photograph the historic bridges of Madison County when he stops by her farm to ask for directions. Her husband and two children happen to be at the state fair for several days. One thing slowly leads to another, and the two have a brief, passionate love affair where the woman gets to finally experience the love of a lifetime. It's incredibly alluring. You find yourself rooting for this woman to experience this joy she's never had. And with Clint Eastwood and Meryl Streep, the acting is excellent. But the problem is, no matter how you dress it up, adultery is evil. It's a terrible sin against your spouse, and it never leads to lasting joy. But *The Bridges of Madison County* powerfully speaks to our hearts to believe otherwise.

This doesn't mean you should never read or watch anything that contains something evil in it. The key question to ask, though, is "Is that evil portrayed as evil?" When we read or watch something that portrays something evil as evil, it can actually deepen our hatred of evil and help to fortify the fear of the Lord in our hearts. The problem comes, however, when something evil is portrayed as good—especially when it is subtly portrayed that way. We must be alert to this because there is a danger that our hearts will be drawn to agree with this portrayal as well. The more we are exposed to it, the more we are tempted to think, "Maybe this isn't so bad after all."

We saw in chapter 6 that the fear of the Lord causes us to detest evil. Conversely, when our hearts become entangled and enamored by evil—when they become corrupted—we find our fear of the Lord weakened. This is why we must attend to our hearts with care and why we must do as the Scriptures teach us: "Keep your heart with all vigilance, for from it flow the springs of life" (Prov. 4:23).

Helping Others Grow in the Fear of God

So those are some important ways for us to grow in fearing God ourselves. But what are the things we can do to help make disciples when it comes to fearing God? How can we help others grow in their fear of the Lord?

Fear God Yourself

It's often said that joy is contagious. Reverence is as well. We pass along what is in our hearts to others, even if it's unconsciously. In the same way that rejoicing in God conveys to others that God is full of gladness and worthy to rejoice in, so our reverence for God conveys to others that he is to be feared. So simply fearing God in the presence of other Christians will help them to fear him themselves.

Don't Treat the Things of God Lightly

We live in an age of flippancy. We've already discussed the fact that there are really no people we reverence, but there's also really no thing or subject we reverence either. Everything is fair game for our jokes, and it seems like we always want to be joking.

Don't get me wrong. Humor is a great thing, and I love to laugh. But when we make a joke out of everything, we'll find that there is nothing we can actually take seriously, and we leave no place for reverence in our lives.

Chapter Ten ▪ 141

Frankly, I think it's wise for us to be overly cautious about making any joke about the Bible or about what takes place in worship service or prayer or the like. Irreverence corrupts our hearts and others' hearts too. If the holy things used in the service of the tabernacle and the temple in ancient Israel were regarded with reverence, isn't it wise to approach the "holy things" in our lives with fear and trembling?

Speak to Others about God's Power and Holiness

Since reverence is kindled in our hearts when we experience power and holiness, we can help others grow in the fear of the Lord by speaking about his power and holiness. Sharing how we've seen God act supernaturally or how he's clearly and powerfully answered our prayers helps to stir reverence in others' hearts for him. When the word goes out about how God has acted in his holiness and his power, the response is the same as it was in the days of the early church: "And great fear came upon the whole church and upon all who heard of these things" (Acts 5:11).

We can also do this by pointing to our recent interactions with the Bible where we've been struck by God's power or holiness or how we've experienced that power or holiness through his work in our hearts or the created world around us. This might require a little thinking in advance of our gatherings with other Christians—before our weekly small group or the coffee we're planning to have to catch up and encourage one another. We might stop and think about (and even jot down answers to) questions like, "Where have I seen or heard about the power of God evidenced lately? How have I experienced God's holiness? In what ways might these things pertain to my friend's life so I can share with them?"

William Wilberforce, the British evangelical and abolitionist who lived at the turn of the eighteenth century, was known to make plans like these before the large dinner parties he would host. He would carefully consider everyone who was coming and what particular questions he might ask or things he could share that would draw them into spiritual conversations that would benefit them. This wouldn't be a bad practice for us to engage in, either, in order to love our brothers and sisters in Christ.

Encourage Others to Think about Just, Pure, Lovely, Commendable, Excellent, or Praiseworthy Things

Paul warns his younger friend and protégé, Timothy, to "avoid irreverent babble, for it will lead people into more and more ungodliness, and their talk will spread like gangrene" (2 Tim. 2:16–17). Likewise, in his letter to the Ephesian church, he tells them, "Let no corrupting talk come out of your mouths, but only such as is good for building up, as fits the occasion, that it may give grace to those who hear" (Eph. 4:29).

Chapter Ten ▪ 143

If hearing, reading, or watching what is evil—even subtly evil—or irreverent has a corrupting effect on a Christian's heart, what is it that strengthens the soul in its love for what is good and its fear of God? Is it only reading the Bible or engaging in explicitly spiritual discussions or worship services? It is, of course, those things, but it's a mistake to think that it's only those things. Paul encourages the Philippian church to a much wider consideration: "Finally brothers, whatever is true, whatever is honorable, whatever is just, whatever is pure, whatever is lovely, whatever is commendable, if there is any excellence, if there is anything worthy of praise, think about these things" (Phil. 4:8).

We live in a world full of stories, acts, and truths that are just, pure, lovely, commendable, excellent, and worthy of praise. We should learn about, read, watch, and think about these things and share them with others. I'll give you an example from one of my very favorite reads last year, *Watership Down*.

If you're not familiar with this story, it's about a group of rabbits who leave their warren at the premonition of one small rabbit that there is a great danger and evil coming. These rabbits, who face a thousand predators, must make their way through woods and wild to find and establish a new home. While there are many things I could say about the book, the one thing I will say is that I don't know if I've ever read a book where the beauty of courage for the sake of others shines forth so clearly. These are, after all, rabbits—and as I'm sure you're aware, the rabbit's one surefire "defense" is essentially to run from the many predators who are stronger and who are fanged and clawed. But these rabbits refuse to leave any behind and risk death time and again for the sake of their friends. It's a beautiful book, and I had the joy of discussing it with about fifteen others at the book club held monthly at my children's school.

These conversations, the opposite of corrupting talk, build others up in their love for God and for what is good. As we've already said, a true love for what is good and the fear of God go hand in hand, the same way that the love of evil and a disgust for God do. So if we want to help others grow in the fear of the Lord, let's think about—and encourage them to think about—what is true, beautiful, and good.

Pastors and Worship Leaders

Hebrews 12:28–29 speaks to the way that the church is to worship God: "Therefore let us be grateful for receiving a kingdom that cannot be shaken, and thus let us offer to God acceptable worship, with reverence and awe, for our God is a consuming fire."

The church's worship service is truly an awesome moment. You are gathering together before the living God, who is "holy, holy, holy" and whose greatness is

Chapter Ten ▪ 145

unsearchable. "Our God is a consuming fire," which means that he "burns up" all unholiness and evil in his presence—he simply cannot tolerate it. If you are a pastor or worship leader, let this reality weigh on your heart as you lead the church in worship.

What does this look like? It doesn't mean you always have to be somber or that there should never be smiles or laughter in the worship service (though there is, of course, a place for grief and lament in our services). But it does mean that the tone of the service—and your leadership in it—conveys that something weighty and serious is taking place in that moment. This is not merely a casual gathering of friends, and it's not a place for flippant jokes. It carries with it the gravity—albeit the seeming paradox of a joyful gravity—of meeting with the great King over all the earth. Lead and preach in this spirit, then: in the fear of the Lord. If you do, that will be conveyed to the hearts of those gathered for worship.

Chapter Eleven

How Do We Grow in Love for Others?

Which one of these is not like the others: Canada, Spain, Mexico, or the USA? I'll give you a second to think (start playing the *Jeopardy* music in your head). You must have it figured out by now—it's Spain, of course, the only country of the four that is not part of North America. I really love answering those kinds of questions and figuring out the connection between three of the items that isn't true of the fourth.

We could play our little game of "odd man out" with the four different foundational motivations of discipleship. Which of these is not like the others: love for God, trust in God, fear of God, or love for other people? "That's easy," someone might say. "It's love for other people because the other three are directed toward God." That's true, but that's *too* easy. Do you know which of the

Chapter Eleven ▪ 147

four is different from the others for a different funda-
mental reason? Cue the *Jeopardy* music again.

Did you come up with the same answer? If you did,
you're right (well, as long as you know *why* you gave
the same answer... didn't you hate it in school when the
right answer wasn't enough for your teacher and you
had to explain why as well?). Love for others is not like
love for God, trust in God, or fear of God. It is indeed
the odd man out.

Here's why—and this is particularly important to
understand in order to grasp how we grow in love for
other people (and how we grow in love, trust, and fear
of God as well).

Growing in love for, trust in, and fear of God are
always a response to seeing, understanding, or experiencing something about God. We see or think about
God's goodness, and we love in response; we see his
faithfulness, and we trust; we see his holiness, and we
fear. Affection love, trust, and fear are always a response,
a reaction to something.

But that's not true when it comes to love for others. In
fact, the love for others to which God commands us—a
joyful resolve for the good of others—is often something
we are to possess despite anything in another person that
would naturally call forth a response of love.

Think of two cars sitting side by side in one of those
crash-test tunnels. Those two cars are going to move
from one end of the tunnel to the other but in different

ways. At the opposite end of the tunnel from one of the cars is a huge magnet, and when the magnet is turned on, it pulls the car toward it. The other car runs the usual way; the engine is cranked and fueled by gasoline as it moves to the other end of the tunnel.

Love, trust, and fear of God are like the car moved by the magnet—the "sight" of God draws them forward. But love for other people is like the other car—it must be fueled by something else. There is no "magnet" in other people that always calls forth our love for them. What is it, then, that fuels our resolve love for others?

It is possible for our love for others—our joyful resolve for their good—to be fueled by our affection love for them. You can probably think of several songs that essentially say, "I adore you so much that I will do anything for you." Or, to give another example, think of the love of a parent whose child is so dear to them that they would die for that child to live. So yes, affection love—delight in another—can fuel resolve love. That's the way God intended it to be in marriage, in the family, and in the church, the family of God. However, affection love by itself is not durable enough to consistently sustain love for others, even in happy marriages, homes, and churches. As human beings, our affections are too fickle for that to be the case. Affection love is like paper thrown onto a fire that causes it to flare up and start to burn again more brightly, but more than paper is needed to keep the fire burning through the night. So, affection love fuels our resolve love, yes. But it's not enough in and of itself.

It's evident that there is no way that affection love can fuel the type of love Jesus commands when he says, "Love your enemies." To have an enemy means there is hostility and dislike between you, not affection. And if we're truthful, we have to admit that we can't even fulfill the command to "love your neighbor"—the people in our workplaces and communities and who live right next door to us—on the strength of our affections for them. So if affection love, though it fuels our resolve love for others at certain times, is not enough, what is?

The Fuel for a Lasting Resolve Love

There is only one source for a resolve love strong enough to endure the ups and downs of life and great enough to encompass even its enemies. That source is God—the God who is love. This supernatural source of resolve love must find its way to the human heart. And God, in his grace, has made a way for this to happen. The Holy Spirit brings about a supernatural change in the human heart and then comes to reside there himself. This is once again the mysterious and powerful work of the Spirit called "regeneration," or being born again.

But it's not as though the Spirit enters our hearts totally unbeknownst to us and then we start to love others out of the blue. No, the Spirit comes and makes us aware of the love of God, and *it's the awareness of his love* that causes us to start loving others—even our enemies! This new, supernatural "birth" comes through hearing the good news of God's love:

> Having purified your souls by your obedience to the truth for a sincere brotherly love, love one another earnestly from a pure heart, since *you have been born again,* not of perishable seed but of imperishable, *through the living and abiding word of God;* for
>
> "All flesh is like grass
> and all its glory is like the flower of grass.
> The grass withers, and the flower falls,
> but the word of the Lord remains forever."
>
> *And this word is the good news that was preached to you.* (1 Peter 1:22–25, italics added)

We are born again through the good news of God's love for us—and for the world—in Christ. It's this awareness of God's love that serves as the fuel for our resolve love toward others. Here's how this works:

The awareness of God's love frees us up from trying to prove our worth (often by competing in some way to be better than others) and provide for ourselves (so we shut others out) so we can look outside ourselves and spend ourselves for the good of others.

Chapter Eleven ▪ 151

The awareness of God's (resolve) love for us causes us to (affection) love him in response. This affection love causes us to want to be like him, because we always aspire to what we admire and delight in. That's the reason my sons designate themselves as their favorite professional athletes when we're playing sports in the backyard. And why my daughter is one Disney princess or another most all the time. Those we admire, we emulate. When our hearts are enthralled with the beauty of God, we strive to be like him in his resolve love. Thus, our love for God fuels our resolve love for others.

Likewise, our awareness of God's love inspires and deepens our trust in him. And our growing trust in God, his promises, and the truth of his word fuels us to love others as well. The more we trust God, the more we are willing to obey God's commands regarding others (thus, loving them), even when those commands contradict our "gut instinct" or natural human wisdom. We love more because we are willing to risk more, banking on God's word rather than our own human wisdom.

Practical Ways to Grow in Love for Others

It's the Spirit dwelling in us, the Spirit who is love working through the love of God for us, who produces the resolve love we have for others. What are some practical things we can do to aid the Spirit's work to grow in our love for others?

Strive to Grow in Loving and Trusting God

The best way to ensure we're growing in our love for other people is to engage in the practices and means of grace we've already discussed that will help us to grow in love for God and trust in him. Whenever you plant a tree, it's inevitable that there will be more oxygen in the air, because the tree produces it. In the same way, when love for and trust in God is "planted" in a human heart, it's inevitable that love for others will be produced.

As we outlined above, the more we relish and savor God, the more we will want to be like him. And God is preeminently love—he delights to do good to others. Thus, the more we grow in our love for God, the more we will grow in gladly doing good to others ourselves. Likewise, the more we trust God, the more readily we will obey his varying commands to love others even in the most trying or difficult circumstances. To see our love for others grow, then, it's critical that we tend and nourish the "tree" of our love for and trust in God.

Love Other People

If we're going to grow in loving other people, we also need to love other people. Yes, you read that right. It sounds paradoxical, but the point is that we grow in love for others not merely by listening to sermons on how glorious love is or by reading books about love but by actually loving others. We've got to *do* something!

We've talked about how awareness of God's love serves as the primary fuel for our love for others. But as we start to actually love others, the act of loving others furthers our growth to love others more too.

This happens because we experience the happiness or blessedness that "it is more blessed to give than to receive" (Acts 20:35). This joy spurs us on to love more and more. Our fallen human nature makes this reality so hard to believe, since we find the opposite assertion firmly lodged in our hearts: "It's better to get for myself than to give to someone else." But there is indeed greater joy in giving than receiving. Every year, we see this when our young kids spend their meager savings to buy their siblings Christmas presents. No matter what they receive, the greatest joy on their little faces always seems to come from watching their brothers or their sister open the gifts they bought for them. Loving others trains us—or retrains us, according to our original design—as we taste this counterintuitive joy.

This also happens because the habit of loving others forms our character so that we become more loving people. The resolve to love others strengthens, and it becomes a reflex—a more automatic response in all the situations we find ourselves in. This will become not just something that we *do* but who we *are*—lovers of other people. It is the formation of character, which the Bible speaks of in Romans 5:4 ("endurance produces character"). Christians are to *characteristically* be lovers of other people, and the way this character is formed is through long force of habit or practice.

Frankly, there is no shortage of opportunities in any of our lives to love other people. These acts of love don't need to be huge or life-altering. They just need to be aimed at doing good to others. Even a person who might be limited to their home still has great opportunities to love others by praying for them.

A bit of intentionality can be helpful here, especially if we are in the early growth stages of becoming lovers of other people. Ask yourself often, "What can I do for him or her that would do them good?" Again, if it's small, that's okay. Doing someone a small amount of good still helps them, glorifies God, and helps you become a more loving person.

So, to grow in your love for others, stop sitting on your hands—do something to love someone today!

Be Committed to and Involved in a Local Church

This means not merely attending services but also being involved in the lives of others in the church. To love other people, you need to be around other people, and the church in particular. These are people who are going to encourage you to love by their example and their words, and whom you are especially commanded to love as a Christian: "By this all people will know that you are my disciples, if you have love one another" (John 13:35). If we remain aloof from the church—from our brothers and sisters in Christ—how can we ever love them like God commands us?

But it's not just out of obligation that we're to be a part of a local church. Outside of perhaps only our families, the church is the best place to learn to love others. While many people have had church experiences that make this statement hard to believe, it's true. In his profound wisdom, God designed it that way. Think about it. The church is a community where we are to speak the truth in love. We're to tell one another the truth, which includes correcting one another when we err so we don't harm ourselves (or others) or dishonor God. It also means being honest about what we think and how we feel. At the same time, everyone is to do this in love, with an eye to seeking others' good. We're called to be patient with one another and bear one another's burdens. And when this goes wrong, God has placed guardrails in place so that the whole project doesn't fall off a cliff and crash. We're to extend grace to one another, be kind and tenderhearted, and forgive one another in Christ the same way he's forgiven us. What better environment could you find to grow in loving others than the church when it functions the way that God designed it? There isn't one.

To cut oneself off from the local church is effectively to cut oneself off from growing as a disciple of Jesus. If there is a genuine local church near you preaching the good news of Jesus and holding to the truth of God's Word, though it be riddled with faults, you need to gather with these Christians.

Dwell in the Reality that You are Justified by Faith

Two large, intertwined obstacles to loving other people are pride and self-righteousness. They come together to form a thorny hedge over the door that leads to loving other people. But there's a sword that's able to slice through them both. This sword will sever the tendency to compare yourself to others, which will free you up to love them. This sword is the clear understanding of what it means to be "justified by faith" and wielding this truth like a weapon.

In Romans 3:19–25, the apostle Paul makes it clear that no person is justified (declared righteous or innocent) by God on the basis of how well they have kept God's law (vv. 19–20). Instead, the only way anyone can be justified is on the basis of Jesus's death, which pays the penalty for all sins, and the means of receiving this justification is simple faith or trust in him. This justification is available to all people, no matter how far short of God's law they've fallen. Glorious!

But then look at the immediate application Paul makes from this amazing truth:

> Then what becomes of our boasting? It is excluded. By what kind of law? By a law of works? No, but by the law of faith. For we hold that one is justified by faith apart from works of the law. (Rom. 3:27–28)

"There is no place for boasting," Paul says, "regarding how well you have kept God's law compared to the Christians around you. You are not justified on the basis of keeping God's law. Everyone who has faith in Jesus stands on the same ground before God, on the righteousness of Jesus's perfect life."

The more aware we are of this, the more it sinks into our bones that there is no competition between Christians to outdo one another in holiness. We can never be more accepted than we are now in Christ. We can never be more loved because of what we do than we are now in Christ. Yes, we can please or displease God by our thoughts and actions, but God's love does not wax and wane with how much we please him. There is no competition with other Christians for God's love or a greater approval from him.

So, Christians no longer have the satisfaction of a smug sense of superiority over other people—that's a sad loss for our sinful nature. But it's replaced by the greater joy of truly rejoicing in the good of other people. I'm not threatened by my Christian brothers' or sisters' growth in holiness. Instead, I'm freed up to rejoice in it as I help them grow. I'm freed up to love them!

When we consider God's wisdom in all this, what can we say but "oh, the depth of the riches and wisdom and knowledge of God!" (Rom. 11:33).

Helping Others Grow in Their Love for Other People

As we've discussed, the way that resolve love for other people originates is different from how love, trust, and fear of God do. It's not a direct response to what we see in other people the way that love, trust, and fear of God are responses to seeing God for who he is. Instead, love for others is fueled indirectly by the Spirit through our knowledge of God and the awareness of his love.

This means that helping those around us grow in their love for other people is a bit more challenging than growing in their love, trust, and fear of God. When we're helping others grow "upwardly" (towards God), we're simply seeking to bring the loveliness or faithfulness or holiness of God before their eyes and hearts. But when it comes to helping them grow "horizontally" (in love towards other people), there's an additional step needed. Seeing God and responding in love, trust, and fear still must be translated into a desire to seek the good of other people. What are some of the ways we can come alongside the Spirit in helping that process take place in the hearts of others?

Ensure Love Is Understood

Given the confusion surrounding love, the first thing we can do to help others grow in love for those around them is to ensure that they understand what love is. It's hard to love other people – and grow in love for other people – if you don't know exactly what love is.

Understanding what resolve love is and that God commands us to this type of love is a necessary first step to actually loving other people.

But it's not only a general understanding of love that's needed. People need help understanding what love requires them to do in particular circumstances. They need help answering the question, "What do I need to do that would be good for this person in this situation?"

Answering this question requires a broad understanding of God's Word. As we've already seen, all of the commands in God's Word related to other people are essentially different ways to love them or do them good (Gal. 5:14). God hasn't left the command merely at "love one another" but has taught us what love looks like in a thousand different ways. Sometimes, it might look like encouragement. Other times, it might look like admonishment (1 Thess. 5:14). In one situation, it means overlooking an offense (1 Peter 4:8). In another, it means confronting a brother or sister who has wronged you (Matt. 18:15). Loving others requires first the knowledge of God's commands, then wisdom and discernment to apply them rightly in our particular circumstances.

Helping others understand love more clearly is a significant way for pastors and teachers to assist those they are discipling grow in their love for other people. But the more that any Christian rightly understands

God's commands, the more he can help others discern what love requires in their specific circumstances.

Affirm God's Love

An awareness of God's love frees us up to love others. It frees us up from the need to prove ourselves to establish a sense of our worth. Instead, we know we're valued because of God's love for us. We no longer have to compete against others to prove we're better than them, but can love and help them instead. An awareness of God's love also frees us up from the anxiety of providing for all our needs. Because we have confidence that God will care for us, we can turn our attention away from ourselves to care for others. The more we sense God's love for us, the more that we will love other people. If this is true, then we can help other Christians grow in their love for other people by consistently affirming the reality of God's love for them.

These affirmations are especially needed because many of us tend to slip back into thinking it's our good behavior that commends us to God. We become proud when we're doing well and downcast when we're not. But a Christian in despair, anxious about her relationship with God, will have trouble loving others. Like a weed that strangles a healthy plant, this anxiety will significantly choke the growth of her love for other people. It will cause her to focus inwardly on the state of her own soul so much that she's rarely able to look outward to others. It's the assurance of God's love in Christ – based on his performance, not ours – that's the antidote for this condition.

Make sure, therefore, that those whom you seek to disciple understand the gospel and remember it throughout the day. Tell them often that God loves them. Remind them of the many Bible verses that speak about the greatness of God's love for his people. In short, do everything you can to point them to the reality of God's love.

Set an Example

Another way to help others grow in their love for other people is to set an example for them yourself. It's easy to discount the influence that our lives have on others, but the Bible makes the power of a godly example clear. In 1 Timothy 4:12, Paul insists that his young protégé, Timothy, serve as an example to others in the church: "Let no one despise you for your youth, but set the believers an example in speech, in conduct, in love, in faith, in purity." And in 1 Corinthians 11:1, Paul urges the Corinthian church to look to his example and imitate it: "Be imitators of me, as I am of Christ."

Setting an example by joyfully loving others ourselves makes it clear to other people that the way of love is possible – and that it's also beautiful. There's nothing quite as compelling to move us to love others as seeing someone full of love for other people. From my own life, I still recall the faithful elderly Christians who were part of the church I grew up in. Their lives of love and joy were beacons that later helped draw me to Christ out of darkness and confusion. They also still inspire me to love others today.

Pray and Encourage

Finally, to help others persevere and grow in love for other people, we can pray for and encourage them as they love others.

Loving others is difficult. It's difficult because of our fallen nature. After years as a Christian, it's discouraging how natural it is to operate in a "me-first" mode. It's astonishing how much effort it takes to wrench your mind from focusing on self to think about others consistently. We need the Spirit to move powerfully to change our hearts and turn them outward to love other people, so we need to pray for others (and have others pray for us).

Loving others is also difficult because of the sinfulness and human frailty of those we seek to love. We need to encourage others to press on amidst the disappointments, hurt feelings, rejection, and hostility – all the messiness that comes with striving to do good to others in a fallen world. So that they don't grow weary in doing good, we need to encourage others often by telling them to "be steadfast, immovable, always abounding in the work of the Lord, knowing that in the Lord your labor is not in vain" (1 Cor. 15:58).

Conclusion

Until the Kingdom Comes

There you have it, friends: a simple model of discipleship. To be a disciple of Jesus means to follow him in loving, trusting, and fearing God and in loving other people. If we grow in these, we will grow as disciples. If we help others love, trust, and fear God and love other people, then we are making disciples.

We've talked at length about what love (in both senses), trust, and fear are. We've also talked at length about the "dynamics" of each of these—how they originate and grow. And finally, I shared some practical things we can do to grow in each of those, as well as how we can make disciples by helping others grow in love, trust, and fear.

There's just one more thing I'd like to share before I close, and that's to remind you that discipleship has an end—and that keeping this end in mind matters.

The End of the Road of Discipleship

When Jesus began his ministry, Mark recorded his first sermon in eighteen words. These eighteen words are some of the most significant ever uttered in all of history: "The time is fulfilled, and the kingdom of God is at hand; repent and believe in the gospel" (Mark 1:15).

What was this gospel (good news)? Was that some other message that Jesus didn't share here, and we need to look elsewhere in the Bible to find? No, it's right there in his sermon: "The time is fulfilled, and the kingdom of God is at hand."

What did that mean? In short, it meant that the world, which had fallen into darkness and evil and had its throne usurped by Satan, had just been "invaded" by one man who had come to overthrow the kingdom of darkness and establish the kingdom of God. He quickly made that clear by the miraculous things he did. Satan's kingdom meant the rule of evil, but Jesus cast demons out. Satan's kingdom was a place where sin separated human beings from God, but Jesus forgave sins. Satan's kingdom was a catalog of sickness, blindness, deafness, and lameness, but Jesus healed them all and made people whole. Life in Satan's kingdom always culminated in death, but Jesus raised the dead.

And then through his own death and resurrection, Jesus made a way for human beings to come into the kingdom of God—to have their sins forgiven and be reconciled to God—but also to have the very life of the kingdom come into their lives through the Spirit of God coming to dwell in their hearts.

Through it all, he reiterated the promise of the Old Testament that one day the kingdom of God would fully come. But that day would not come as soon as Jesus's disciples anticipated. Instead, it was God's plan for his kingdom to be established quietly, slowly, and incrementally, not immediately and fully after Jesus's resurrection.

But one day, the kingdom will come in its fullness. Jesus will return, and his work of making all things new will be complete. All evil, pain, grief, death, sin, and selfishness will be purged from this world, and it will be a "new heavens and a new earth in which righteousness dwells" (2 Peter 3:13). And all who dwell in it will live in a society of perfect love for God, trust in God, fear of God, and love for one another.

Why This Matters

Discipleship is about growing into the people we will one day be when the kingdom of God comes in its fullness. Being a disciple is like being a sapling that's maturing into a full-grown tree. That sapling *will* one day be a tree, just like one day, dear brother or sister of faltering love, trust, and fear, you *will* be made perfect in all of these.

This truth keeps us from seeing discipleship as just some sort of regimen for spiritual fitness or practices we need to engage in to grow as Christians. We have a fixation in America (to say the least) with physical fitness and health, and we are constantly harping (and being harped on) about all the practices we need to engage in to stay in good health. This also extends to our fascination with "life hacks," countless clever things that make our lives easier. While I'm not (wholly) knocking this, I am saying that there is danger of this mindset bleeding over into our spiritual lives so that we see discipleship as a bunch of "spiritual life hacks" to maximize the fullness of this life here and now. Again, it's not all bad to maximize the fullness of our lives here and now. But the problem is that where we fail to see a connection between this life and the life to come, our commitment is only so strong.

I could offer my own level of commitment to the gym as exhibit A. I know I need exercise to stay physically healthy, and sometimes my resolve for that exercise is strong and I'm at the gym consistently. Other times, my resolve is… not as strong. And I have many (good?) justifications for not going to the gym, but at the end of the day I know the reality is that I'm not going to be physically healthy forever. I can invest as much as I want at the gym, but someday the bottom is going to fall out of that investment.

But our spiritual lives are not merely one more aspect of our lives in this world; they are who we will eternally be. This is exactly the point that Paul makes in 1 Timothy 4:7–8: "Train yourself for godliness; for while bodily training is of some value, godliness is of value in every way, as it holds promise for the present life and also for the life to come." We do well, then, to be reminded of this often and having this reality spur us on to strive toward that day.

This truth also teaches us another important lesson—don't despair about where you are as a disciple. Examine yourself, yes. Grieve and repent where there is sin, unbelief, and slothfulness. But you must not despair as if you will never change, as if there is no hope. If you are in Christ, you are the complete opposite of hopeless. God has promised—promised!—that he will finish the work of making you like Christ: "He who began a good work in you will carry it on to completion until the day of Christ Jesus" (Phil. 1:6 NIV).

He *will* carry it through to completion. Though you are just a sapling now, by the power of God you will be an oak tree one day. Don't forget that; be encouraged and press on!

Until the kingdom comes, then, may you experience the richness and fullness of a life full of loving, trusting, and fearing God and loving other people!

Personal Reflection and Small Group Discussion Guide

I've written this guide to help individuals reflect more deeply on the book as well as to serve as a discussion guide for small groups who are reading the book together.

I would strongly encourage anyone using the guide to answer the pre-reading questions before reading each chapter. Often, this question is the same big question that's asked in the title of the chapter. But I believe that having the reader wrestle with their answer to this question and put it into words before reading what the author has to say is extremely beneficial. We always learn more when we're forced to wrestle with a subject before someone else tells us what they think about it. Taking the time to answer these pre-reading questions will impress the material more deeply on your heart and make your discussions livelier.

Personal Reflection and Small Group Discussion Guide ▪ 169

Since many of the sets of questions close with a self-evaluation question, I would encourage the reader (or the small group) to conclude each set by responding to God in prayer.

Introduction: A Simple Model of Discipleship

Pre-Reading Questions
Why are you reading this book? What do you hope to gain from it? What questions about discipleship do you hope it will answer?

Post-Reading Questions
1. What is the simple model of discipleship that the author shares?
2. What does he mean by calling it a model? How is it simple?
3. How long have you been a Christian? Which category that the author mentions (new Christian, ministry leader, etc.) do you fall into? How well do you feel you understand discipleship?
4. What aspects of discipleship seem puzzling to you? (What a disciple is, how to grow as a disciple, how to make disciples, etc.)

Chapter One: What Is Discipleship?

Pre-Reading Questions

Is the term "discipleship" used frequently in your church? What do you think most church members understand it to mean? What do you understand it to mean?

Post-Reading Questions

1. The author states that most of the teaching he's heard on the broad topic of discipleship frames the conversation around two big questions: "What is a disciple?" and "How do we make disciples?" Is this also true in your experience? If not, how have you heard discipleship taught?

2. Why is it not enough to say that we are to follow Jesus in Christlikeness?

3. Why do we have trouble answering the question, "In what ways are we to follow Jesus?" How does this simple model of discipleship overcome that obstacle?

4. What does the author list as the four foundational motivations in the Lord's heart? Are there any others that come to your mind? Is it possible that what you're thinking of flowed out of one of the four foundational motivations the author lists?

172 ▪ *A Simple Model of Discipleship*

5. Why doesn't this book talk much about the practices related to discipleship? Where is the best place to learn and talk about these? Is this happening in your life?

6. How does this chapter help clarify the concept of discipleship for you? What questions do you still have?

Personal Reflection and Small Group Discussion Guide ▪ 173

Chapter Two: What is Love?

Pre-Reading Questions
How would you define love? How do you think our society would define it?

Post-Reading Questions
1. The author stated that love is not one thing but two things—that is, we use the word in two different ways. What are those two ways?
2. Whom or what do you love with affection love?
3. Do you tend to think of affection love as less significant than resolve love? Why?
4. What Scriptures come to mind that use "love" in the sense of affection love? What Scriptures come to mind that use "love" in the sense of resolve love?
5. How is love both two simple things and one compound thing?
6. Has this chapter changed your understanding of love? If so, how?

174 ▪ *A Simple Model of Discipleship*

Chapter Three: What Does It Mean to Love God?

Pre-Reading Questions
What do you think it means to love God?

Post-Reading Questions
1. How does loving God relate to obeying God?
2. The author says that the "temperature" of our love for God is to be very warm—that is, almost exclusively affection love. Do you agree? What Scriptures convince you (or lead you to disagree)?
3. The author likens our love for God to a person deeply in love. Why do you think many men think of this type of love as strictly feminine? Why is this seeing it incorrectly?
4. Has this chapter changed your understanding of what it means to love God? How?
5. After reading this chapter, how would you evaluate your love for God?

Personal Reflection and Small Group Discussion Guide ▪ 175

Chapter Four: What Does It Mean to Love Other People?

Pre-Reading Questions

How would you respond if someone asked you, "What does it mean to love other people?"

Post-Reading Questions

1. What "temperature" should our love for others be? Which Scriptures make this clear to you?
2. What's the difference between the way Christians are commanded to love those outside the church versus those inside the church? Which Scriptures make this clear to you?
3. Do you think loving our enemies is one of the crying needs of the day for Christians in America? Why?
4. Has this chapter changed your understanding of what it means to love other people? How?
5. After reading this chapter, how would you evaluate your love for other people?

176 ■ *A Simple Model of Discipleship*

Chapter Five: What Does It Mean to Trust God?

Pre-Reading Questions
What does it mean to trust God? What is it specifically about God we are to trust?

Post-Reading Questions
1. To become a Christian means coming to trust in Jesus. What is it about him we must trust?
2. If we've already trusted Christ in order to become Christians, how is it possible for us to grow in trust?
3. The author discussed how Jesus's prayer in the garden of Gethsemane demonstrated his perfect trust in God. What other passages from the Gospels make this trust clear?
4. What are the three things the author lists that we must trust about God? Which one of these seems most difficult for you? Why do you think that's the case?
5. Which promises of God are for Christians today? What dangers do you see from an answer that's too broad ("every promise made in the Bible is for me") or too narrow ("only the promises made specifically to Christians or the church in the New Testament are for me")?

Personal Reflection and Small Group Discussion Guide ▪ 177

Chapter Six: What Does It Mean to Fear God?

Pre-Reading Questions
How would you explain what it means to fear God?

Post-Reading Questions
1. How is it possible to both fear God and love him?
2. Does the fear of the Lord include terror of him? Why or why not?
3. How does Exodus 20:18–21 help us to understand the fear of the Lord?
4. What is similar about discipline and punishment? What is different?
5. What are the three ways the fear of God looks in our lives? In which of these ways do you see the fear of God working out in your life? In which ways does it seem to be lacking?

Chapter Seven: What about Growing in the Knowledge of God?

Pre-Reading Questions

To this point, the author hasn't mentioned anything about growing in the knowledge of God. Where do you think that fits into this simple model of discipleship?

Post-Reading Questions

1. In your mind, do you equate Bible knowledge with spiritual maturity? Have you ever known someone with significant Bible knowledge yet little Christlikeness?

2. Bible knowledge isn't everything, but it is essential. Why?

3. Knowledge is an awareness of something that is true and an accurate perception of a certain aspect of reality. What are the two types of knowledge? How have you experienced each type recently?

4. Why is the first type of knowledge vital to our spiritual lives? Why is the second?

5. Which type of knowledge do you think matters more when it comes to discipleship? Why?

6. How does reading this chapter affect the way you will seek to know more about God?

Personal Reflection and Small Group Discussion Guide ▪ 179

Chapter Eight: How Do We Grow in Love for God?

Pre-Reading Questions
How do you think affection love usually grows?

Post-Reading Questions
1. What are the three ways that affection love grows? Through which of them do you seem to experience the strongest affection love?
2. Think about (and share, if you're in a small group) a "moment of glory" in God that you've experienced. How did it affect your love for God?
3. Which of the repeated pleasures in God that the author shares do you find especially stirs your heart to love God? Which has done so recently?
4. Which of the four habits listed is the most difficult for you to practice regularly? How does seeing these practices as a means of experiencing greater love for God help with that?
5. Which temptation to sin poses the greatest danger to extinguishing the fire of your love for God?
6. What specific ways can you help others grow in their love for God?
7. What practices do you need to put in place (or recommit to) after reading this chapter?

180 ▪ *A Simple Model of Discipleship*

Chapter Nine: How Do We Grow in Trust in God?

Pre-Reading Questions
How does trust in someone or something grow?

Post-Reading Questions
1. Think about a trusted friend or family member. Think about how you came to trust them. Do you see parallels to your relationship with God?
2. Which passages of the Bible have especially strengthened your trust in God?
3. How has attending worship services and spending time with other Christians helped your trust in the Lord to grow?
4. Which of God's promises has been sweetest to you? How have you seen God at work in your life to keep this promise?
5. What stories of God's faithfulness to you do other Christians need to hear so their trust in him will grow?
6. Think of two or three friends going through a challenging time. What promises from God could you share with them to help them trust him more in their specific circumstances?
7. Which practices do you need to put in place (or recommit to) after reading this chapter?

Personal Reflection and Small Group Discussion Guide ▪ 181

Chapter Ten: How Do We Grow in Fear of God?

Pre-Reading Questions
How do you think reverence for another person grows?

Post-Reading Questions
1. Is there a person in your life that you revere (rightly and deeply respect)? How did you come to have that reverence for them?
2. What are the two characteristics that cause us to grow in reverence?
3. Is regularly attending worship services helping you to grow in your fear of God? If so, how? If not, why do you think that's the case?
4. Both God's Word and his world help us to grow in our fear of him. Which of these has impacted your life most powerfully recently? Do you need to spend more time in either of them?
5. Think about what you've been watching or reading lately. Is good being portrayed as good in it, and evil as evil? How is this affecting your fear of God?
6. In which specific ways can you help others grow in the fear of God? What just or commendable or lovely things can you encourage others to think on?
7. What practices do you need to put in place (or recommit to) after reading this chapter?

182 ▪ *A Simple Model of Discipleship*

Chapter Eleven: How Do We Grow in Love for Others?

Pre-Reading Questions

How does our love for other people grow?

Post-Reading Questions

1. In what significant way does love for others differ from love, trust, and fear of God?

2. What is it that fuels a lasting resolve love for others? How? Have you experienced this personally?

3. How does loving other people help us to grow in love for other people? How have you seen this happen in your life?

4. Is your local church a place where Christians have plenty of opportunities to love one another? What are those opportunities? If there aren't many, what could you do to provide more?

5. The author writes of "two, large intertwined obstacles" to loving other people. What is the "sword" that slices through them both? How does it do so?

6. Consider the four ways that were shared as far as helping others grow in their love for other people. Which of these are you best gifted and equipped to do? What are some specific ways you could engage in these practices this week?

7. What practices do you need to put in place (or recommit to) after reading this chapter?

Personal Reflection and Small Group Discussion Guide ▪ 183

Conclusion: Until the Kingdom Comes

Post-Reading Questions
1. What is the end of the road of discipleship?
2. Why is it important to keep this end in mind?
3. How does keeping this end in mind help you personally?

Acknowledgments

Thank you to all those who took the time to read the early drafts of my manuscript. Not only was your feedback helpful but your enthusiasm encouraged me to believe that what I've written will benefit others.

Thank you to Tobi Carter (cover and interior designer), Meaghan Markus (copyeditor), and Liz Smith (proofreader) for making this book read and look much better than it would have otherwise. Since the final responsibility in all these areas was mine, the blame lies with me instead of them for any shortcomings.

Thank you to my church family. Without your encouragement and the richness of what we've shared together in Christ over the past decade and a half, I seriously doubt this book would have been written.

Thank you, Dad and Mom, for your unfailing love and support. And for always making sure there was enough money to buy me books every month in elementary school.

Thank you, Beckett, Pax, Knox, and Mercy, for the joy you bring me as your dad. What you've cost me in sleep you've more than made up for in happiness. As the years pass, I hope that what I've written returns that favor as it helps to deepen your joy in Jesus.

Thank you, Talona, for listening patiently every time I asked for your opinion on my latest writing dilemma. And there were a lot of times. I love you—in other words, I greatly delight in your beauty, and I'm joyfully resolved for your good.

Most of all, thank you, God—Father, Son, and Spirit—for reaching into my life and giving me hope when I had none. Thank you—for everything.

CPSIA information can be obtained
at www.ICGtesting.com
Printed in the USA
BVHW061211110121
597454BV00004B/21